# HORSE *Laffs*

## A Collection of Equine Humor

for brother-in-law Bill
and Kathain K. Vance
award "winning" humor!

## Les Vance

In memory of my grandfather Paul Harris who farmed
the hills of English Ridge with draft horses.
Two of his favorites were Jim and Bill.
He cared deeply for his animals.


In memory of my own horse Springtown Garibaldi (AMHA 140660)
AKA Mighty Mikey the Mischievous Morgan.
He was a horse with a sense of humor.

# Acknowledgements

If you own horses, by definition, you have a sense of humor. If you can't laugh at yourself, you learn. Few of the observations, stories, and jokes (most humorous, others, not so much) in this book are original. Most were found on the web where they have been circulating--many of them--for years. Before that, they were heard in stables, race tracks, show grounds, and the feed store. Wherever horsemen and women congregated, there was always some jokester who thought he deserved more laughs than he got.

Fortunately, many made their way to electronic form. Initially shared via email among those few who had access to internet email or a bulletin board system. In 1979, Usenet was created by a couple of North Carolina grad students, a distributed internet discussion system that provided "news groups" in which users could read and post messages. It predated the web by a decade. Without going into the technical details, Usenet was the prototype social networking platform. The news group rec.equestrian, was one of the first on Usenet. It provided a way for horse people to socialize without having to jump in their pickup trucks and drive someplace where they could meet to share advice and stories. The stable, more often than not was that place. Although it doesn't see as much traffic these days, rec. equestrian is still an active community. The topic of a recent discussion thread was the perennial diesel vs. gasoline engine argument. Which is the least expensive way to drive between equestrian gatherings? Most of the humor circulating in rec.equestrian eventually found its way onto the web, which is where I found it.

In academic circles, the kind I run in these days, it is said that plagiarism is stealing from one person and research is stealing from many. Well then,

I'm a wanted man in all fifty states and several foreign countries. I searched every nook and cranny of the web for equine stories and jokes but I'm sure I missed more than I found. Much of the material was found duplicated on several websites. Often, with minor variations, additions, deletions, etc. So I did some editing. Judiciously, I hope. Errors in judgment about what to include are my own (there's no accounting for taste). As are any failures in attribution to the correct sources.

I'm confident, though, that Emily and Megan, two young dressage riders, are the authors of the Top Ten Ways to Know Your Dressage Test Needs More Work and Ten (More) Ways to Know Your Dressage Test Needs Work. Knowing nothing beyond their first names and ages when these were written (whenever that was), I earnestly hope that they continue to be the kind of horsewomen who take their sport seriously, but with the same astute sense of humor that enable them to draw immense enjoyment from their equine partnerships. Annamaria Tadlock is the author of You Know You are an Equine College Student When. Scooter Grubb's observant contribution: Living with Obsessive Compulsive Equine Attachment Neurosis Syndrome is guaranteed to elicit nods of knowing agreement. The poem "When I Am old" is found in several versions. Humorous? Not exactly. However, the reader can easily visualize her twinkling eyes surrounded by crinkly laugh lines. Evidence of a lifetime smiling, chuckling over equine antics, and growing in wisdom. The kind of wisdom that lingers just beneath the surface of the very best humor.

If you can help identify sources for the material you find here, I'd like to know. I'll be sure they're incorporated in the next edition. And if you've heard any new jokes, be sure to send them along. I could use a good laugh while I'm researching and writing. My website is www.lesvance.com.

If I had to choose a favorite equine joke, it is this one:
A horse walks into a bar. Orders a beer. The bartender asks, "why the long face?"

# The Beginning of the End

A friend gives you a horse. . . . . . . . . . . . . . . . . . . . . . . . .

You build a small shelter. . . . . . . . . . . . . . . . . . . . .$750.

You fence in a paddock. . . . . . . . . . . . . . . . . . . . . .$450.

Purchase small truck to haul hay . . . . . . . . . . . $12,000.

Purchase a 2 horse trailer. . . . . . . . . . . . . . . . . $2,800.

Purchase 2nd horse. . . . . . . . . . . . . . . . . . . . . . $2,500.

Build larger shelter with storage . . . . . . . . . . . . . $2,000.

More fencing . . . . . . . . . . . . . . . . . . . . . . . . . . . $1,200.

Purchase 3rd horse . . . . . . . . . . . . . . . . . . . . . . $3,000.

Purchase 4 horse trailer. . . . . . . . . . . . . . . . . . $17,500.

Purchase larger truck . . . . . . . . . . . . . . . . . . . $23,000.

Purchase 4 acres next door . . . . . . . . . . . . . . . . $38,000.

More fencing . . . . . . . . . . . . . . . . . . . . . . . . . . . $2,000.

Build small barn. . . . . . . . . . . . . . . . . . . . . . . . $18,000.

Purchase camper for truck . . . . . . . . . . . . . . . . . $9,000.

Purchase tractor . . . . . . . . . . . . . . . . . . . . . . . $23,000.

Purchase 4th & 5th horse. . . . . . . . . . . . . . . . . . $6,500.

Purchase 20 acres . . . . . . . . . . . . . . . . . . . . . . $285,000.

Build house . . . . . . . . . . . . . . . . . . . . . . . . . . $185,000.

Build barn . . . . . . . . . . . . . . . . . . . . . . . . . . . . $56,000.

More fencing & corrals . . . . . . . . . . . . . . . . . . $24,000.

Build covered arena . . . . . . . . . . . . . . . . . . . . $182,000.

Purchase crew cab dually . . . . . . . . . . . . . . . . . $44,000.

Purchase gooseneck w/living quarters . . . . . . . . $45,000.

Purchase 6th, 7th & 8th horse . . . . . . . . . . . . . $10,750.

Hire full time trainer . . . . . . . . . . . . . . . . . . . . $50,000.

Build house for trainer . . . . . . . . . . . . . . . . . . . $84,000.

Buy motor home for shows . . . . . . . . . . . . . . . $125,000.

Hire attorney -- spouse leaving you for trainer . . $35,000.

Declare bankruptcy, spouse gets everything.

Friend feels sorry for you . . . . . . . . . . . .gives you a horse.

# And God Created the Horse

On the first day of creation, God created the Horse.

On the second day, God created Man to serve the Horse.

On the third day, God created all the animals of the earth to spook the Horse when Man was upon his back.

On the fourth day, God created an honest day's work so that Man could labor to pay for the keeping of the Horse.

On the fifth day, God created the grasses in the field so that the Horse could eat and Man could toil and clean-up after the Horse.

On the sixth day, God created veterinary science to keep the Horse healthy and Man broke.

On the seventh day, God rested and said this is good.

# Equine Dictionary

---

**Auction**: A popular, social gathering where you can change a horse from a financial liability into a liquid asset.

**Azoturia**: A condition brought on by showing horses all weekend. Symptoms include the feeling of dread at having to get out of bed on Mondays and go to work. (See Monday Morning Disease)

**Barn Sour:** An affliction common to horse people in northern climates during the winter months. Trudging through deep snow, pushing wheelbarrows through snow and beating out frozen water buckets tend to bring on this condition rapidly.

**Big Name Trainer:** Horse owners follow them blindly, will gladly sell their homes, spend their children's college funds and their IRA's to support them, as they have a direct link to The Most High Ones (Judges).

**Bit:** What you have left in your pocket after you've been to your favorite tack shop.

**Bog Spavin**: The feeling of panic when riding through a marshy area. Also used to refer to horses who throw a fit at having to go through water puddles.

**Bolt:** To gulp food usually occurs with sandwiches at half-hour holds.

**Bran:** A wheat by-product occasionally fed moistened to horses, most usually applied as spackle or stucco on owner.

**Colic:** The gastrointestinal result of eating at the food stands at horse shows.

**Colt:** What your mare always gives you when you want a filly. (See Filly)

**Contracted foot:** The involuntary/instant reflex of curling one's toes up right before a horse steps on your foot.

**Corn:** Small callus growths formed from the continual wearing of cowboy boots.

**Cribbing:** The vice of chewing your pencil while doing the budget and worrying about the cost of next year's hay.

**Cult Leader:** See Big Name Trainer.

**Dog House:** What you are in when you spend too much money on grooming supplies and pretty halters.

**Drench:** Term used to describe the condition an owner is in after he administers mineral oil to his horse.

**Endurance ride:** The end result when your horse spooks and runs away with you in the woods.

**Equitation:** The ability to keep a smile on your face and proper posture while your horse tries to crow hop, shy, and buck his way around a show ring.

**Easy to Catch:** In a 10x10 stall.

**Easy to Load:** Only takes 3 hours, 4 men, a 50lb bag of oats, and a tractor with loader.

**Easy Rider:** Rides good in a trailer; not to be confused with "ride-able".

**Feed:** Expensive substance utilized in the manufacture of large quantities of manure.

**Fences:** Decorative perimeter structures built to give a horse something to chew on, scratch against, and jump over. (See inbreeding)

**Filly:** What your mare always gives you when you want a colt. (See colt)

**Flea-bitten:** A condition of the lower extremities in horse owners who also own dogs and cats.

**Flies:** The excuse of choice a horse uses so he can kick you, buck you off, or knock you over. He cannot be punished.

**Founder:** The discovery of your loose mare—some miles from your farm—usually in a flower bed or cornfield. Used like-"Hey, honey, I found'er." A condition that happens to most people after Thanksgiving dinner.

**Frog:** Small amphibious animal that emits a high-pitched squeal when stepped on.

**Gallop:** The customary gait a horse chooses when returning to the barn.

**Gates:** Wooden or metal structures built to amuse horses.

**Girth Sores:** Painful swelling and abrasion made at the point of one's mid-section by fashionably large western belt buckles.

**Green Broke:** The color of the face of the person who has just gotten the training bill from the Big Name Trainer.

**Grooming:** The fine art of brushing the dirt from one's horse and applying it to your own body.

**Grooms:** Heavy, stationary objects used at horse shows to hold down lawn chairs and show bills.

**Hay:** A green itchy material that collects between layers of clothing, especially in unmentionable places.

**Head Shy:** A reluctance to use the public restrooms at a horse show. Always applies to pit toilets.

**Head-Tosser:** A blonde-haired woman who wears fashion boots while working in the barn.

**Heaves:** The act of unloading a truck-full of hay.

**Hives:** What you get when receive the vet bill for your 6 horses, 3 dogs, 4 cats, and 1 donkey.

**Hobbles:** Describes the walking gait of a horse owner after his/her foot has been stepped on by his/her horse.

**Hock:** Financial condition of all horse owners.

**Hoof Pick:** Useful, curved metal tool utilized to remove hardened dog doo from the tread of your tennis shoes.

**Horse Auction:** What you think of having after your horse bucks you off.

**Horse Shoes:** Expensive semi-circular projectiles that horses like to throw.

**Inbreeding:** The breeding results of broken/inadequate pasture fencing. Unsuccessful line breeding.

**Jumping:** The characteristic movement that an equine makes when given a vaccine or has his hooves trimmed.

**Lameness:** The condition of most riders after the first few rides each year; can be a chronic condition in weekend riders.

**Lead Rope:** A long apparatus instrumental in the administration of rope burns. Also used by excited horses to take a handler for a drag around the arena.

**Line Breeding:** Breeding of related horses to improve the quality of offspring. (See inbreeding)

**Lunging:** A training method a horse uses on its owner with the purpose of making the owner spin in circles-rendering the owner dizzy and light-headed so that they get sick and pass out. The horse can go back to grazing.

**Manure Spreader:** Horse trader.

**Monday Morning Disease:** See Azutoria.

**Mosquitoes:** Radar equipped blood sucking insects that typically reach the size of small birds.

**Mustang:** The type of horse your husband would gladly trade your favorite one for. Preferably in a red convertible with a large V-8.

**Overreaching:** A descriptive term used to explain the condition your credit cards are in by the end of show season.

**Owner:** Human assigned the responsibility for feeding horses.

**Parasites:** Small children that get in your way when you work in the barn. Many gather in swarms at horse shows.

**Pinto:** A colorful (usually green) coat pattern found on a freshly washed and sparkling clean grey horse that was left unattended in his stall for ten minutes.

**Pit Crew:** Absolutely indispensable people occasionally noted for their ability to get lost, be in the way, eat all the food, or be sleeping in the camper when you finish a 100 mile ride.

**Pony:** The true size of the stallion that you bred your mare to via transported semen that was advertised as 15 hands tall.

**Proud Flesh:** The external reproductive organs flaunted by a stallion when a horse of any gender is present. Often displayed in halter classes.

**Quarter Cracks:** The comments that most Arabian owners make about the people who own Quarter Horses.

**Quittor:** A term trainers have commonly used to refer to their clients who come to their senses and pull horses out of their barns.

**Race:** What your heart does when you see the vet bill.

**Rasp:** An abrasive, long, flat metal tool used to remove excess skin from the knuckles.

**Reins:** Break-away leather device used to tie horses with.

**Ringworms:** Spectators who block your view and gather around the rail sides at horse shows.

**Sacking out:** A condition caused by Sleeping Sickness (see below). The state of deep sleep a mare owner will be in at the time a mare actually goes into labor.

**Saddle:** An expensive leather contraption manufactured to give the rider a false sense of security. Comes in many styles. All feature built-in ejector seats.

**Saddle Sore:** The way the rider's butt feels the morning after the weekend at the horse show.

**Sleeping Sickness:** A disease peculiar to mare owners while waiting for their mares to foal. Caused by nights of lost sleep, symptoms include irritability, red baggy eyes and a zombie-like waking state. Can last several weeks.

**Splint:** An apparatus that can be applied to various body parts of a rider due to the parting of the ways of a horse and his passenger.

**Stall** What your truck does on the way to a horse show, fifty miles from the closest town.

**Tack Room:** A room where every item necessary to work with or train your horse has been hidden.

**Twisted Gut:** The feeling deep inside that most riders get before their classes at a show.

**Three Gaited Horse:** A horse that. 1) trips, 2) stumbles, 3) falls.

**Versatility:** An owners ability to shovel manure, fix fences and chase down a loose horse in one afternoon.

**Vet Catalog:** An illustrated brochure provided to stable owners that features a wide array of products that are currently out of stock or have been dropped from a company's inventory.

**Weaving:** The movement a horse trailer makes while going down the road with a rambunctious horse in it.

**Whip Marks:** The tell-tale raised welts on the face of a rider-caused by the trail rider directly in front of you letting a low hanging branch go. Also caused by a wet or dry horse tail across the face while cleaning hooves.

**Windpuffs:** Stallion owners. Also applied to used-car salesmen.

**Withers:** The reason you'll seldom see a man riding bareback.

**Yearling:** The age at which all horses completely forget the things you taught them previously.

**Youngstock:** A general term used for all equines old enough to bite, kick, or run you over, but not yet old enough to dump you on the ground.

**Zoo:** The typical atmosphere around most stables.

# Handbook for Horses

---

**Chewing:** Make a contribution to the architectural industry. Chew on your stall wall, the fence, or any other wooden item.

**Children:** Human children require much nurturing in order to develop a healthy self-ego. Never offer your right-lead canter to an adult rider. However, permit the child the honor of the right lead. Older children may be denied the first one or two canter cues, in order to prepare them for adulthood. Very young children MUST be given the right lead on the very first try.

**Death:** When one of your best turn-out friends has gone to the Great Pasture in the Sky. Your human attendant will require much comforting, as they themselves fear that they will go next. Humans are instinctively afraid of death. Offer your comfort by making deep hacking and wheezing coughs that produce voluminous amounts of phlegm. Your human will be greatly comforted, knowing that he's not the next one to go.

**Dining Etiquette:** Always pull all of your hay out of the hay rack, especially right after your stall has been cleaned, so you can mix the hay with your fresh bedding. This challenges your human, the next time they're cleaning your stall. And we all know how humans love a challenge (that's what they said when they bought you as a two-year old, right?).

**Doors:** Any door, even partially open, is always an invitation for you and your human to exercise. Bolt out of the door and trot around, just out of reach of your human, who will frantically run after and chase you. The longer it goes on, the more fun it is for all involved.

**Farrier:** The farrier is an object on which you can take out your frustration without danger of limiting your food supply.

**Fresh Bedding:** It is perfectly permissible to urinate in the middle of your freshly bedded stall to let your humans know how much you appreciate their hard work.

**Ground Manners:** Ground manners are very important to humans; break as much of the ground in and around the barn as possible. This lets the ground know who is boss and impresses your human.

**Holes:** Rather than pawing and digging a BIG hole in the middle of the paddock or stall and upsetting your human, dig a lot of smaller holes all over so they won't notice. If you arrange a little pile of dirt on one side of each hole, maybe they'll think it's gophers. There are never enough holes in the ground. Strive daily to do your part to help correct this problem.

**Humor:** Humans possess a thing called a "sense of humor." This is a delightful emotional sensation that is caused by the sight or sound of things that are out of the ordinary. You can facilitate this by providing unusual situations to trigger the laughter response. On the first day of a 3-day weekend, when your attendant shows up with some of his turn-out buddies, fart loudly, then fall to the ground and stick your tongue out. The sights and sounds you provide will stimulate the necessary laughter response.

**Improper Shoes:** Your human attendant will often risk his safety by wearing shoes that might not provide full protection from hazardous ranch situations. You can correct (not punish) this behavior by applying pressure to the unprotected foot. Humans are known to move away from pressure, but only after making loud noises. Keep pressure applied until your human responds correctly to this cue.

**Long Trail Rides:** Rules of the road: When out for a trail ride with your owner, never relieve yourself on your own lawn.

**Marriage:** Your personal human attendant may also have a spouse, who professes no equinity. Whenever your attendant brings the non-equus spouse to visit, you are to lavish unimaginable amounts of charm on the non-equus spouse, and more importantly, you must act fearful of your personal human attendant. This process must continue until such time as the non-equus spouse converts to full equinity, or "teases" your attendant with a 2X4, as a prelude to the mating ritual.

**Neighing:** Because you are a horse, you are expected to neigh. So neigh. A lot. Your owners will be very happy to hear you protecting the barn and communicating with other horses. Especially late at night while they are sleeping safely in their beds. There is no more secure feeling for a human than to keep waking up in the middle of the night and hearing you, "Neigh, neigh, neigh..."

**Nuzzling:** Always take a BIG drink from your water trough immediately before nuzzling your human. Humans prefer clean muzzles. Be ready to rub your head on the area of your human that you just nuzzled to dry it off, too.

**Playing:** If you lose your footing while frolicking in the paddock, use one of the other horses to absorb your fall so you don't injure yourself. Then the other horse will get a visit from the mean ol' vet, not you!

**Rain:** Humans are generally little busy bodies, like beavers, who need to constantly build and modify. During the rain, stick either your head or butt beyond the reach of your roof. Your human will instinctively (being the stimulus/response creatures that they are) move you to a new stall, and make a new roof for you later.

**Shoeing:** Humans are creatures driven by instant gratification. After a good foot trimming or shoeing, trot smartly around afterwards to show your human how nice the shoes fit. The next day, drag one foot when you walk, to provide your little busy body with yet another project to work on.

**Shots**: Humans are characteristically nervous when providing veterinary care for you. In order to soothe your human, raise your head immediately after the injection; turning the lead rope into a handy tool with which to swing your human. Genetically predisposed, humans are comforted by swinging back and forth on the lead rope while howling like an injured simian.

**Snorting:** Humans like to be snorted on. Everywhere. It is your duty, as the family horse, to accommodate them.

**Stomping Cats:** When standing on cross ties, make sure you never—quite—stomp on the barn cat's tail. It spoils all the fun.

**Visitors:** Quickly determine which guest is afraid of horses. Rock back and forth on the cross-ties, neighing loudly and pawing playfully at this person. If the human backs away and starts crying swoosh your tail, stamp your feet and nicker gently to show your concern.

# Helpful Hints for the Horseman

Don't ever buy a horse expecting it to be your last one.

Don't buy a horse from anyone who keeps telling you how honest they are.

An honest horse trader is one who says: "He's cheap, but he's worth it."

No matter how much you love a car or boat, it will never love you back.

The most valuable horse in your barn isn't the one that cost the most, but the one you love the most.

You may never find a horse that has everything you want, but you'll find a lot that don't have everything you don't.

When you go to look at a horse for sale, don't drive your Mercedes.

It's almost impossible to visit a tack shop without buying something.

There are many horses who are loved more by the heart then by the eye.

People who have horses often live a long time without getting old.

Treat all of your horses as if they all cost $100,000.

When someone asks you if you think their new horse is wonderful just say yes.

When you ALMOST fall off, get kicked or have a piece of tack break, it's often better than all the advice in the world.

You'll learn more about riding by getting on different horses than from reading all the "how to" books in existence.

A dime is still good for something; you can tighten the latch on your trailer with one.

Telling a child how wonderfully they ride might make them feel good, but it will never teach them anything.

Your true test of patience will come when everyone has gone home and your horse won't load in the trailer.

Nothing brings a prayer to your lips more quickly than racing down a steep hill with a wide ditch at the bottom.

If you keep searching for the perfect horse, you will be searching for a long time.

A good test of your character is how you treat your horse when no one is around.

Not even the finest instructor in the world can guarantee you'll know everything about riding after a year's worth of lessons. Or 10 years. Or 100 years.

It's grand to be a better rider than other people--just don't keep telling them.

# Top 10 Things You Need to Know if You Own a Horse

To induce labor in a mare? Take a nap.

To cure equine constipation? Load them in a clean trailer.

To cure equine insomnia? Take them in a halter class.

To get a horse to stay very calm and laid back? Enter them in a liberty class.

To get a mare to come in heat? Take her to a show.

To get a mare in foal the first cover? Let the wrong stallion get out of his stall.

To make sure that a mare has that beautiful, perfectly marked foal you always wanted? Sell her before she foals.

To get a show horse to set up perfect and really stretch? Get him out late at night or anytime no one is a round to see him.

To induce a cold snap in the weather? Clip a horse.

To make it rain? Mow a field of hay.

# Things your Horse Can Teach You

---

When you are angry, let me teach you how well I can stand on my hind feet because I don't feel like cantering on my right lead today.

When you are worried, let me entertain you with my mystery lameness.

When you feel superior, let me teach you that—mostly—you are the wait staff.

When you are self-absorbed, let me teach you to PAY ATTENTION. Remember how I told you about those lions hiding in the woods waiting to turn us into a snack.

When you are arrogant, let me teach you what 1200 lbs of "YAHOO LETS GO!" can do when suitably inspired.

When you are lonely, let me be your companion. Let's do lunch. Also, breakfast, afternoon tea, and dinner.

When you are tired, don't forget the 600 lbs of grain that needs to be unloaded.

When you are feeling financially secure, let me teach you the meaning of "Veterinary Services."

When you want to learn, hang around, Bud. I'll learn ya.

# Fun Stall Activities

---

**Poop in the water game:** This will test your coordination and spatial abilities. Horses all over the world practice this, every day. You must try to poop in your water container (note: drink water first, so you won't go thirsty!). If your water container is too high to poop in, you can attempt to poop on the stall's door, or on the wall. This also gives your human something to do. When they see what you've done, they will marvel at your special abilities, then happily provide you with fresh water.

**Pee in the water game:** A real challenge for geldings and stallions. Attempt to pee in your water container. This is a very challenging game. If your water container is up against a wall, you may try to drag it into the middle of your stall. If your human is dull and fails to realize that you've peed in your water, simply dump it out and they will refill it. This in itself can actually be a game, called the Dump Out Your Water game.

**Artistic Wood Carving:** You can become a wood carver. Use your teeth to chisel the wood of your stall into a beautiful piece of art! At first, you can start with simple shapes—such as the half-moon bite shape—and as you become more advanced you can try different forms (big curve shape or multiple bite shapes). Your human will really appreciate this. Some humans will actually remove your artwork from the stall, and put up fresh, new, unchewed boards, encouraging you to develop your artistic abilities with a fresh, new canvas!

**Grain Spilling Game:** Try to dump out all of your grain from your grain bucket/container, by turning it over with your nose. It is a fun game. You can even continue to flip the container to be sure that all the grain is dumped on the ground. Then, using your delicate muzzle to guide you, try to pick up all the grain, sorting through the bedding and poop. Amusing, and it makes your grain last longer. Your human will appreciate it too. He/she may even bring you a new bucket of grain, or challenge you to become better by using more difficult containers.

**Hay Dunking:** In this game, you'll try to grab a bite of hay, carry it to your water container, and dump it in. Dropping hay in your water is fun for both you and your human! Although it's just hay, they will probably come into your stall and remove it from your water (then you can dump more in). This gives humans something to do.

**Who Can Be The Loudest:** If you're stabled with other horses, try a little friendly competition with this game. When it's feeding time, see who can neigh, bang, scream, and kick the loudest in their stalls. Humans will instinctively throw food to the noisiest, most demanding horse, so try to be it. The winner is the horse that the human feeds first.

**Smoosh The Bedding:** In this game, you can attempt to mix your bedding, poop, and hay all together. You do this by walking all around in your stall, until you get a good, even mixture. Some horses walk in circles, or back and forth in a straight line. Experiment with different styles to see which you like best. Again, this provides entertainment and exercise for your human, because they will have to clean it all up.

**Roll in the stall:** Attempt to get a good roll in your stall. If your stall is big, this is easy; however, the smaller the stall, the more difficult it becomes. The object is to roll without getting stuck. There is some danger in this game, as you could roll up near a wall and get stuck. If you get stuck, make sure you thrash loudly so that your human will notice you, nearly have a heart attack, then come to your rescue. This game is best played when humans are around.

**Mane Rubbing:** Try to rub your mane out in certain spots. Humans like neat manes. That is why they comb, spray, and pull your mane. Save them work by pulling your mane yourself! You can stick your head through the stall (if it has an opening) and try to rub the top of your neck. Or, just rub it on the side of a wall. This will give your mane a nice look that humans appreciate (clumps of hair missing). You'll save them time on having to pull your mane or trim a bridle path.

**Unique Pooping:** This not only provides fun for you, but fun for the human as well, because it makes the regular boring task of mucking more interesting. Try pooping in unusual areas. Poop on top of your door latches, or poop on window ledges. Poop in any food containers, or on top of salt licks. Try to poop any place that is not the ground.

# What You See vs. What Your Horse Sees

**Blowing Paper:** At any moment it could whip up into our faces, covering our noses. We could suffocate. And don't try to tell me you'd do CPR.

**Barking Dogs:** What? You've never read Steven King's CUJO?

**Puddles of Water:** Quicksand.

**Trash Cans:** They've been known to swallow horses and transport them into another dimension.

**Babies and Little Kids:** Long lost tribe of horse-eating pygmies.

**Plaid Horse Blankets:** Hey, when was the last time you wore plaid? It adds 100 lbs.

**Ropes and Hoses:** Dreaded North American Trail Snakes.

**Ponies:** Cute, clever, hardy. They want to take over the world.

**Windy Days:** Two Words: impending tornado.

**Carts and Wagons:** Look. You put a human on our backs; we can always buck them off. But hitching a horse to a wheeled object? It's just wrong.

# The Herd Outcast

A stick with a few dead leaves on it can make very scary noises. Take advantage of this fact.

Plastic bags can also be quite scary to other horses.

So can large pieces of rubber.

Well, Ok, pretty much anything can appear frightful when held in the mouth and shaken. It is fun to chase around other horses using this knowledge.

Other horses also seem to be quite scared of loud noises. A hoof against metal works quite well.

Coughing loudly behind an unsuspecting horse can also be quite effective.

Most horses do not know what to think when you stand on your hind legs for more than 5 seconds at a time.

Most horses also do not know what to think when you climb into the salt feeder.

Or the grain feeder.

Neither do most people.

Any open object is meant to be climbed into. Never mind the size of the object in comparison to your size.

Also never mind that the object may be harder to exit than it was to enter.

Trailers are more fun to get into than they are to get out of. Do not consider this fact when entering the trailer. Strongly consider it when asked to get out.

Horse hair bears a striking resemblance to grass.

So does people hair.

All objects have the potential to be edible. Much taste-testing and chewing is required to discover this potential.

Other horses make interesting noises when you nip them.

Especially when you nip them on the butt.

Especially when the horse you are nipping is a female.

People make interesting noises when your place your foot on theirs.

People also make interesting noises when you buck while they are sitting on your back.

The higher the buck, the louder the noise.

If you possess a large, hangy-down thing, then you are a stallion, no matter what the vet did to you.

Be sure everyone knows that you are a stallion.

Mares find stallions very attractive. Remind them of this as often as possible. Ignore any rude remarks, or respond with one of the above techniques for regaining control of the herd.

Food was meant to be eaten and water was meant to be drunk. Nothing can change this fact. The more barriers in the way, the more this applies.

Water is also meant to be splashed in.

And rolled in.

These acts are more fun when someone is sitting on your back.

If something is fun without an audience, it is twice as fun with an audience.

The larger the audience, the greater the fun.

Bits were made to be chewed on. They were not made as a device to control you.

Ditto with halters.

And lead ropes.

"Good boy!" should be music to the ears. Respond to this phrase with pricked ears and a happy face. This phrase always applies to you.

Come to think of it, "good boy" is the only phrase that always applies to you.

Unless you are a mare.

"No" does not apply to you. Ever. Neither does "naughty" or any similarly negative phrase.

Be sure your slave knows that these phrases do not apply to you and you do not appreciate any negative attitudes.

"Whoa" applies to you only when you are tired of moving.

"Giddyup" applies only when you are tired of standing.

Under opposite circumstances, each can easily be misinterpreted as the other.

In fact, most phrases can easily be misinterpreted to your liking.

Rules were meant to be broken.

Unless they are rules that you wrote.

Then they should be applied as often as possible.

In as many different circumstances as possible.

As long as possible.

And the possibilities are endless.

# A Horse's New Year's Resolution

I CAN walk and poop at the same time—I can, I can, I can!

I will NOT stop and poop or urinate every time I pass the same spot in the arena.

I will NOT leave when my rider falls off.

My stall is NOT my litter box. When I have free access to my paddock, I will NOT go back inside to pee.

I will NOT roll in streams or try to roll when my human is on my back.

I will NOT leap over large non-existent obstacles when the whim strikes.

I will NOT walk faster on the way home than I did on the way out.

I promise NOT to swish my tail while my human is cleaning my back feet.

I also promise NOT to choose that particular time to answer nature's call.

I will NOT bite my farrier's butt even if he had corn flakes for breakfast.

I will NOT confuse my human's blonde hair for really soft hay.

I will NOT wipe green slime down the back of my human's white shirt.

I will NOT blow my nose on my human.

I will NOT try to mooch goodies off every human within a one mile radius.

I will NOT lay totally flat out in my stall with my eyes glazed over, tongue hanging out, and my legs straight out and pretend I can't hear my human frantically screaming "Are you asleep?"

I will NOT chase the ponies into the electric fence to see if it is on.

I promise NEVER to dump the wheelbarrow of manure while my human is mucking my stall.

I will NOT grab my lead rope in my mouth and attempt to lead myself.

I will NOT have an attitude problem. I won't, I won't, I won't!

I will NOT pull my new shoes off the very next day just to prove that I can.

I am neither a beaver nor a carpenter. I promise I WON'T eat or remodel the barn or the new fences.

I am NOT a battle steed. I will not act like one.

I WILL forgive my human for the very bad haircut, even though I look like a freak.

I accept that not every carrot is for me.

I will NOT do the Arab Teleport Trick when a bad/naughty/awful horsa-saurus monster is hiding behind the closest tree.

I will NOT jump in the air and turn 180 degrees every time I see a deer.

I will understand that deer are NOT carnivorous.

I will NOT shy at familiar objects just for fun.

I will NOT bite the butt of the horse in front of me during the trail ride just to say "Hi".

I WILL put my ears forward and cooperate when it comes to photos.

# Top 10 Things You Won't Hear Your Horse Say

---

Don't clean out my stall, I adore the aroma.

No thanks, one can of oats is enough for me.

Doctor, may I please have a rectal exam.

I just love traveling in a hot trailer.

Mr. Farrier, please don't stop pounding on my hooves.

There's room for one more on my back.

I feel like galloping another 20 miles.

Low branch! Duck!

You can go ahead and leave, I'll wash myself down.

Can we do this again tomorrow?

# All I Need to Know in Life I Learned from My Horse

---

When in doubt, run far, far away. Then graze.

You can never have too many treats.

Passing gas in public is nothing to be ashamed of.

New shoes are an absolute necessity every 6 weeks.

Ignore cues. They're just a prompt to do more work.

Everyone loves a good, wet, slobbery kiss.

Never run when you can jog. Never jog when you can walk. And never walk when you can stand still and graze.

Heaven is eating for at least 10 hours a day... and then sleeping the rest.

Eat plenty of roughage.

Great legs and a nice rear will get you anywhere. Big, brown eyes help too.

When you want your way, stomp hard on the nearest foot.

In times of crisis, take a poop.

Act dumb when faced with a task you don't want to do.

Follow the herd. That way, you can't be singled out to take the blame.

A swift kick in the butt will get anyone's attention.

Love those who love you back, especially if they have something good to eat.

# Misclassified Advertisements

---

Appleloosa for sale.

Willingly piaffes & massages.

Bay 3-yr-old, lightly started, lounges well.

Cooked semen available.

Welsh filly, pretty head & eye. Just stared over fences.

3-yr-old TB mare, recently startled under saddle.

Aged race gelding, has four clean kegs.

Rider must sell: horse going to college.

Gray pony, very athletic, broke to dive.

Small horse farm for sale, 33 acres, large fenced pastures plus three small haddocks.

Attractive gelding for combined training, ready to brake in the spring.

Warmblood mare, no lices. Reasonably priced to good home.

Registered Hockey Club mare.

Super mover—gloats over the ground.

Always in the ribbons over fences & thunder saddle.

Select young stock for sale, top scores at insurrection.

Oldenburg colt, will manure to 17 hands.

Young Hanoverian, started u/s, bumping over small courses.

LFG-Live Floral Guarantee.

# Some Crosses We'd Like to See

Quarter Horse + Halflinger: Three-Quarter Horse

Quarter Horse x Halflinger: Half Quart

Quarter Horse x Buckskin: Quarter Buck

Quarter Horse x Warmblood: Warm Horse

Paint x Palomino: Paint Pal

Fjord x Gypsy Vanner: Ford Van

Mustang x Bashkir: Mustache

Foxtrotter x Irish Hunter: Fox Hunter

Halflinger x Jutland: Half Jug

Miniature Horse x Foxtrotter: Mini Fox

Saddlebred x Appaloosa: Saddleloosa

Gotland x Appaloosa: Gotloose

Appaloosa x Danish Warmblood: Apple Danish

Oldenburg x Saddlebred: Old Saddle

Thoroughbred x Suffolk: Rough Folk

Tennessee Walker x Friesian: Walking Freezer

Pinto x Warmblood: Pint Blood

Welsh x Shetland: Wetland

# Horse Reality Shows

---

**Survivor, the Endurance Ride:** Ten elite show riders leave their oak tack trunks, their minimum wage grooms, their canopies, and gooseneck living quarters behind to spend 2 days in Death Valley. They have to perform heinous acts such as cleaning their own tack, grooming and caring for their own horse, and getting along with other riders. As we sit back and watch riders succumb to this torture, the strongest break away from camp in search of a cell phone, golf cart and bottled mineral water.

**I'm a Dressage Queen, Get Me out of Here**: A Prix St. Georges rider and her Hanoverian stallion are shipped to a working cattle ranch. In Episode 3, she ruins her full seat Eurostar breeches while closing the cattle gate. Unable to ride until her new attire is shipped, the local wrangler round pens her horse and starts roping off his back.

**Joanne Millionaire:** Rich young women are first introduced to the exciting world of horses. They become completely hooked on the finest purebreds, the best trainers, fabulous stabling, and expert instruction. In the last episode, they discover they are penniless.

**N/H Trainers in the City**: Two young, hip, good-looking round pen trainers share a New York apartment as they learn about life, work, & love in the city. In the pilot episode, Patrick gets arrested after slapping his chaps at a girl who won't turn & face him (she turns out to be an undercover cop), and Roger ends up in the emergency room after trying to round-pen his new girlfriend's Siamese cat.

**American Show Idol**: Thousands of equestrians must audition in front of exacting judges who pick apart their ride using colorful evaluations such as "try tennis!" and "clucking to your horse makes you sound like a chicken." George Morris guest stars.

**Matched by America**: Contestants who are tired of looking for Mr. or Ms. Equine Perfection allow the studio audience to vote on which horse is truly the best partner for them. Tossing breed and color preferences to the wind, contestants discover that 1) a good horse can be any size, age, color, or breed. 2) When you find the right match, there can be happy endings.

# Horse Traders

---

"The horse you sold me last week is a fine animal, but I can't get him to hold his head up."

"Oh, it's because of his pride. He'll hold it up as soon as he's paid for."

A farmer was trying to sell his horse. After exercising it, he exclaimed to his potential buyer: "Don't you admire his coat?"

"Coat's all right", said the prospect, "but, I don't care for the pants."

A boy went to the horse sale and stated, "I want to buy a horse for my mother."

"Sorry," said the salesman, "we don't do exchanges."

A prospective buyer looks over Attaboy and could find nothing wrong with the horse. He asked the owner, "How come you want to sell him so cheap?"

The owner said, "I'm bored with him. He's a show-off. He's an actor. When they take his picture after a win, he turns his profile. When they play a fanfare, he starts to dance. He even whinnies to music."

The prospective buyer said, "Those antics could be cute. I'll buy him."

The owner said, "Okay, Attaboy, get up and do your 'lame' impression."

The farmer was out in his field trying to get another season of plowing from his old horse when all of a sudden this enterprising city slicker came by in his Lincoln Navigator. Slamming on his brakes, he rammed it into reverse and came back to the farmer. He said, "Nice looking horse you got there, want to sell him?"

The farmer couldn't hold back his joy, the words just leaped out of his mouth, "Ya, fifty bucks." The dude peeled off a fifty and yelled he would be back the next day with a trailer. The farmer couldn't contain his excitement. The old horse had been around for years and he only paid ten bucks for him. A dream come true.

The next day at dawn the farmer and horse were at the same spot near the road, when to his amazement the old horse coughed once and keels over dead as a hammer. Just about that time here comes the Lincoln. The city guy was right there with the trailer. He gets out of his SUV and after seeing what's happened, didn't hesitate. Asked the farmer to help load the dead horse on the trailer. Puzzled the farmer obliged and soon the city slicker, Lincoln, trailer and dead horse were all gone.

Just so happened the next month, while in town, the farmer spotted the same guy. The man came over, shook his hand, patted him on the back and gave him another fifty dollar bill. The puzzled farmer asked what happened, the man said he made $645.00 on the deal. The farmer asked him how he did that. The city guy said he sold the horse in a raffle. The farmer said, "Didn't they get mad?" The city slicker said, "Heck no, just the one, and I gave him back his dollar."


"How's life?" asked Mike.

"Couldn't be better", answered Erik enthusiastically. "I have a horse. A very special horse. It does all the housework, cooks, serves me my meals, washes the dishes. He even does the laundry."

"Wow! Your horse is really something. I'll pay you $10,000 for it."

"Nah..." Erik rejected the offer. "I haven't been this spoiled in years."

Next time they met Mike was curious. "What's up these days?"

"Life is beautiful. My horse...I showed it where the supermarket is. It buys my groceries, takes my suits to the dry cleaners. Does all the bothersome errands".

"I double my offer" said Mike. "Would $20,000 be fair?"

"Nah, No offer will be fair enough. I like the way I live now."

The third time they met, Erik couldn't stop praising his horse: "It goes to the office for me. I spend most of my day at the country-club."

"Aaaaahh" Mike was frustrated. "I'll give you $100,000 for your horse. I need this kind of horse!"

"Hmmm... I don't know, Mike, I kinda like my horse, but $100,000... That's a lot of money. You know what? Okay... I'll sell you my horse".

Two months later, Mike met Erik again.

Angrily, Mike exclaimed, "You thieving horse-trader! This horse... it does no housework... it doesn't go to the supermarket like you said, it smells bad, it nibbles my furniture... it's worthless...it's..."

"Hey Mike", Erik calmed him down, "if you continue to bad mouth your horse, you'll never be able to sell it."


One horse-trader said bitterly to the other: "That horse you sold me is blind."

To which the other replied, "Well, I said he was a fine horse but he didn't look good."


A traveling salesman stopped alongside a field on a country road to rest a few minutes. The man had just closed his eyes when a horse came to the fence and began to boast about his past.

"Yes sir, I'm a fine horse. I've run in 25 races and won over $5 million dollars. I keep my trophies in the barn." The salesman computed the value of having a talking horse, found the horse's owner and offered a handsome sum for the animal.

"Aw, you don't want that horse," said the farmer.

"Yes I do," said the salesman, "and I'll give you $100,000 for the horse."

Recognizing a good deal, the farmer said without hesitation, "He's yours."

While he wrote out his check, the salesman asked, "By the way, why wouldn't I want your horse?"

"Because," said the farmer, "he's a liar. He hasn't won a race in his life."

"The horse I bought from you died."

"What? He never done that before."

When asked what he would sell a certain horse for, the Vermont farmer startled the inquirer by naming a price of $1,000. The buyer said he was prepared to pay no more than $100.

"That's a lot less, but I'll take it," said the farmer.

When the deal was done, the buyer asked the farmer why he had come down so quickly from $1,000 to $100.

"Well," drawled the farmer, "just thought it would be nice for you to own a thousand-dollar horse."

A horse trader sold a pair of horses which he guaranteed were willing horses. Shortly afterwards the buyer came back and complained that the horses were very poor workers and added, "You told me that the horses were willing."

"I did," said the trader, "and they are willing: One is willing to stop, and the other is willing to let him."

The old farmer took his horse to a sale.

Someone asked, " Why is that horse so nervous?"

To which the old man replied, "He ain't ever been around this many horse-thieves and liars before."

# Honest Harry's Horse Sales

"Alright folks, step right up! You don't want to pay $3.79 for a gallon of gasoline? Want to reduce your contribution to global warming? Be part of the solution instead of the problem. Equines are the perfect transportation solution...completely carbon-neutral. They convert hay and water into 100% natural fertilizer, perfect for your organic garden."

**Trail Horse**: Your average run around town animal. Has the energy to get where you are going, the brain to find the best way to go, and big enough to carry the normal sized American.

**The Arabian**: Perfect for those who travel long distances in a day and try to multitask while driving. Although the Arabian may not go to your home or office without specific instruction, it WILL go somewhere.

**The Draft**: Calling all soccer moms. This big guy can carry the whole team, their gear, and snacks. Just like a full-size van, this guy will require more fuel, and his shoes will be more expensive than the compact model, but the back seat won't be as cramped!

**The Western Pleasure**: The right car for high end white collar workers. This animal works harder and requires more special knowledge so only the best can figure this out. Be sure to take your cell phone. You won't be stuck in traffic, you just won't be getting anywhere fast.

**The Parelli**: Stay at home moms, salesmen, and high school kids will all enjoy this dream. You can load him down with flapping Wal-Mart bags, ask him to walk in places a horse won't fit, and you can dance with him as you listen to the latest tunes.

**The Ranch:** The most dependable animal available. He will go where ever you ask him to, at whatever speed is appropriate. You can tie him to the stop sign and he will be there when you get back. Best of all, this model has been specially engineered to be able to go without water for days and stay fat and slick by eating sagebrush and dead prairie grass.

Of course all models are available in base colors (sorrel, bay, black) Special order colors are available (dun, gray, palomino) and for an additional fee, custom paint jobs are also available (overo, tobiano, blanket, leopard).

No horse is sold with a warranty, however maintenance plans are available in the event brakes, steering, or accelerator fail.

# A Letter to Tech Support

Dear Tech Support,

Recently I purchased and installed Horse 1.0. I soon noticed that this program appears to have numerous glitches. For instance, every time my computer boots up, I have to run Feed 5.3 and Water 7.1. Many times I've been in the middle of writing an important document, and a window will flash telling me to run Clean Stall 2.0. This program also contained applications I did not wish to install, such as Manure 8.5, however they auto-installed with Horse 1.0. Applications such as Vacation 2.7 and Free Time 10.1 no longer run, crashing whenever selected. Possibly the worst is that Horse 1.0 has attached itself to programs like Quicken and MS Money, with folders added such as "Monthly Shoeing" and "Winter Blanket". Periodically, I'll get a reminder telling me to send a check to the manufacturer of Horse 1.0 for the aforementioned items. I have tried to uninstall Horse 1.0 numerous times, but when I try to run the uninstall program, I get warning messages telling me that a deadly virus known as "Withdrawal" will infect my system. Please Help!!!!!

THE REPLY:

Dear User,

Your complaint is not unusual. A common misconception among users is that Horse 1.0 is a mere "utilities and entertainment program." It is not - it is an OPERATING SYSTEM and is designed by its author to run everything! A warning will soon be printed on the box. Since you have already installed Horse 1.0, here are a few tips on how to make it run better. If you are annoyed by the applications Feed 5.3 and Water 7.1, you may run C: \HIRE_HELP, however this will cause another folder to be added to financial applications, labeled "Staff". Failure to send payment to "Staff" will result in Feed 5.3 and Water 7.1 being run again on startup. A note of caution: NOT booting up your computer for several days isn't the solution to avoiding Feed 5.3 and Water 7.1. You will find that, when you boot up your computer again, a nasty virus called "Colic 4.2" will have attached itself to important documents and the only way to rid your computer of Colic 4.2 is by purchasing and installing "Vet 10.1", which we admit is extremely expensive, but crucial. Otherwise, Colic 4.2 will cause irreversible damage to the operating system. Finally, it is important that you run C:\Carrots and C:\Scratch_Ears on a fairly regular basis to keep the application running smoothly. If you have any more questions, please call our toll-free number.

Sincerely, Tech Support

# Welcome to Horseaholics Anonymous

---

Good Afternoon. I am a horseaholic. I would like to welcome all of you to this month's meeting of Horseaholics Anonymous. Some of you are here tonight because a friend or relative, as part of an intervention, brought you. You may be sitting here thinking that you are OK and don't really need any help. It is not easy to admit that you are a horseaholic and it is even harder to bring yourself to an HA meeting for help. HA is here to assist you. I have some questions to ask. If you can answer YES to more than three of the following, you have come to the right place.

Can you say "sheath" in public without blushing?

Do you drive a big truck with a towing package when all your other friends drive Toyotas?

Do you have more than one vehicle? One for you and one for the horses?

Do you spend your holidays going to shows, clinics and seminars while your next-door neighbors take a cruise?

If you do go overseas, is it to a riding vacation in Ireland or to Spruce Meadows to watch the Grand Prix?

Do you discuss things at the dinner table that would make most doctors leave in disgust?

Do you consider formal wear to be clean jeans and freshly-scraped boots?

Is your interior decorator State Line Tack?

Was your furniture and carpeting chosen with your horses in mind?

Are your end tables really tack trunks with tablecloths thrown over them?

Do you know the meaning of _____?

Does your mail consist primarily of horse catalogs and magazines?

Do you get up before dawn to ride? Go to horse shows? Clinics? But have trouble getting up for work?

If you do have dresses, do they all have pockets? Do those pockets often contain bits of carrot, hay, and sweet feed?

When you meet a new person do you always ask them what kind of horse they have and pity them if they don't have one?

Do you remember the name of their horse sooner than you remember their name?

Do you find non-horse people boring?

If you answered YES to only one of the above, there is still hope.

If you answered YES to two, you are in serious trouble.

My advice to all of you with three or more YES's is to sit back and smile, turn to the smiling person next to you, and know that your life will always be filled with good friends and good horses and it will never be boring.

# IF You Do Any of the Following You are Without a Doubt a True Horsewoman

You use your horse's mane/tail comb to put up your hair.

You use your horse's braiding bands for your own hair.

Your horse has more grooming supplies than you have cosmetic products

Your entertainment for the week is moving the manure pile.

You fight for which wheelbarrow you're going to get.

You give your horse more baths than you get yourself.

Your horse has more blankets than you do clothes.

You clip your horse more often than you shave your legs.

You spent more money on a single pair of your horse's front shoes than you did on all your own shoes put together.

You don't have air conditioning, but you have two fans for your horse's stall.

You go to a horse show rather than going to church.

You wear the same dirty clothes every day, so you don't have to make another outfit dirty.

# Identification of the Female Equestrian

Easy to locate, she's either off on the horse or out in the barn.

Upholds the double standard. Smooches with the most bewhiskered beast, but recoils when hubby needs a shave.

Owns one vacuum cleaner and operates it exclusively in the barn.

A culinary perfectionist: checks every section of hay for mold but doesn't blink when she petrifies dinner in the microwave.

Easy to outfit: no need for embarrassing visits to uncomfortable little boutiques. You can find all she wears at your local tack store.

Features a selective sense of smell. Bitterly complains about hubby's sticky-sweet cigar smoke, while remaining totally oblivious to the almost visible aroma of her barn boots drying next to the heater.

A master at multiplication: she starts with one horse, adds a companion, and if it's a mare, she breeds it.

Socially aware: knows that formal occasions call for clean boots.

Easy to please: a new wheelbarrow, custom boots, or even a folding hoof pick will win her heart forever.

A social butterfly: providing the party is given by another horsewoman. Falls asleep in her soup at all other functions.

Economy minded: Won't waste money on permanents, facials, or manicures.

Occasionally amorous: but never leaves lipstick on your collar, at worst, slight trace of Chapstick.

Unmistakable in a bathing suit: She's the one whose tan starts at the nose, ends at the neck, and picks up again at the wrists

A dedicated club woman: As long as the words "horse" or "riding" appear in its name.

Has your leisure at heart: Eliminates grass cutting by turning every square inch of lawn into pasture which, in turn, converts itself into mud.

Keeps an eagle eye on the budget. Easily justifies spending six hundred dollars on new show outfit, but croaks when you blow ten on bowling.

An engaging conversationalist: Can rattle on endlessly about training or breeding.

Socially aware: Knows that formal occasions call for clean boots.

A moving force in the family: House by house, she'll get you to move closer to horse country (and farther away from your job.)

Sentimental fool: Displays a minimum of six 8x10 color photos of the horse in the house and carries a crumpled snapshot of you (taken before you were married) somewhere in the bottom of her purse.

Shows her affection in unusual ways: If she pats you on the neck and says "you're a good boy," believe it or not, she loves you.

# Husbands vs. Horses

## Advantage: Husbands

Husbands are less expensive to shoe than horses.

Feeding a husband doesn't require anything that even mildly compares with the hassle of putting up hay.

A lame husband can still work.

A husband with a bellyache doesn't have to be walked.

Husbands don't try to scratch their heads on your back.

They are better able to understand puns.

If they are playing hard to catch, you MAY be able to run them down on foot.

They know their name.

They usually pay their own bills.

They apologize when they step on your toes.

No saddle-fitting problems.

They seldom refuse to get into the vehicle.

They don't panic, running and yelling all through the house when you leave them alone (unless you've left the kids with them too!).

For a nominal fee, you can hire someone else to clip them.

They don't like the lady next door just as well as you because she fed him for 3 days straight.

## Advantage: Horses

If they don't work out you can sell them.

They don't come complete with in-laws.

You don't have to worry about your children looking like them.

You never have to iron their saddle pads.

If you get too fat for one, you can shop for a bigger one.

They smell good when they sweat.

You can repair their "clothes" with duct tape.

You can force them to stay in good physical condition, with a whip if necessary.

They don't want their turn at the computer.

They may turn white with age, but never go bald.

They have never heard of PMS.

They learn to accept restraint.

They don't care what you look like as long as you have a carrot or an apple.

# Wives vs. Horses

---

## Advantage: Wives

Your wife can feed herself if you have to leave town.

You can (usually) kiss your wife's neck without worrying about getting your feet stepped on.

You can shop for a new car without worrying about whether it's powerful enough to haul your wife.

If you call in sick at work to stay home and play with your wife, there's very little risk of serious injury that will be tough to explain to the boss the next day.

Your wife won't go roll in the mud right before an occasion when she needs to look her best.

Your wife can groom herself much better than you can.

Bathing your wife can be much more entertaining than bathing your horse, and doesn't require tying her up (unless you're into that).

If your wife loses a shoe, you can be pretty sure she has plenty of replacements in the closet.

Your wife's mane doesn't need to be pulled.

## Advantage Horses

Horses are less expensive to shoe. They'll happily wear the same set for weeks.

Horses are less expensive to clip, and one clip job may last all winter.

Your horse won't constantly ask you if his blanket makes his butt look big.

Your horse won't worry about whether his shoes match his saddle.

Your horse won't complain if you occasionally ride a different one.

You have more options for working out your horse's behavioral problems.

Your horse won't sulk if you forget his birthday.

Your horse's farts make yours seem like no big deal.

Your horse won't tell all his friends about every little mistake you make.

Your horse won't constantly nag you to redecorate the barn.

If your horse runs away from you, you can usually get him back.

# Reasons Why Riding is Better than Sex

You don't have to sneak your riding magazines into the house.

If you are having trouble with riding, it's perfectly acceptable to pay a professional to show you how to improve your technique.

The Ten Commandments don't say anything about riding.

If your trainer takes pictures or videotapes of you riding, you don't have to worry about them showing up on the Internet when you become famous.

Your horse won't keep asking questions about other horses you've ridden.

It's perfectly respectable to ride a horse you've never met before, just once, or, ride many horses in the same day, whether you know them or not.

When you see a really good horse, you don't have to feel guilty about imagining riding him.

If your regular horse isn't available, he/she won't object if you ride another horse.

Nobody will ever tell you that you can go blind if you ride by yourself.

When dealing with a riding instructor, you never have to wonder if they are really an undercover cop.

You don't have to go to a sleazy shop in a seedy neighborhood to buy riding stuff.

You can have a riding calendar on your wall at the office, tell riding jokes and invite co-workers to ride with you without getting sued for harassment.

There's no such thing as a Riding Transmitted Disease.

If you want to watch horses on television, you don't have to subscribe to a premium cable channel.

You don't have to be a newlywed to plan a vacation primarily for the enjoyment of riding.

# Why I Like My Horse (Much) Better Than My (ex) Husband

A horse will never ask to borrow money.

When a horse hangs out with his buddies, they usually stay out of jail.

A horse will never call you up (drunk) at 2:30 am and ask for a ride home.

Horses are physically incapable of grabbing the remote control and keeping it.

A horse will never tell you that you cooked his dinner wrong.

A horse will never tell you that he's got another girl.

Very few bill collectors will call and ask for your horse.

A horse is unaware of football, baseball, basketball, or golf seasons.

A horse doesn't know any four-letter words.

Horses do not have to be forced to trim the lawn.

# Saying These Things Anyplace but the Barn May Get in Trouble

He was about 6 months old when we branded him.

He needs a good 20 minute warm-up.

Her baby started walking about 20 minutes after birth.

Don't jump on him, sit down gently.

Has anyone seen my breast collar?

He didn't try to run away when we drove in the nails.

He goes outside in just a blanket.

He had a bad attitude, so we castrated him.

He really over-reacts when I sit down into him.

He has so much stamina, you can ride him all day long.

I know she's going to have a baby soon because her butt is soft.

I rode yesterday, but Suzy's riding him today.

If her baby nurses too hard she bites it.

If he's not good, just grab his lip and twist it.

If he's spilling his food on the ground, he might need a dentist.

More leg, less hand.

Relax your back, don't pinch with your knees. Go with the motion, Rock your pelvis.

She likes to roll in the dirt after her bath.

Smack him with the crop if he refuses to jump.

She has a really nice, big, square butt.

There's nothing like 17 hands between your legs.

When he gets excited he really foams up.

When I'm done riding him, you can have a turn.

# How to Know That Martha Stewart Has Been in Your Barn

There is a potpourri pomander hanging from each halter.

The horse's hooves have been trimmed with pinking shears.

The horse treats are all stored in McCoy crocks.

The manure fork has been decorated with raffia.

That telltale lemon slice in each new silver water bucket.

You find carrot & apple treats stamped out with copper cookie cutters and decorated with royal icing using a #2 rosette tip.

Mane & tail hair has been collected and put into wire baskets for nesting material for the birds.

A seasonally appropriate grapevine wreath adorns the front of each stall.

Your horse goes outside naked and comes in wearing a thyme colored virgin wool hand knitted blanket with matching leg wraps.

The manure pile has been sculpted into swans.

# The Best Reasons to Ride Dressage

Found ice-fishing too stimulating.

Enjoy wearing full formal wear rain or shine.

Who wouldn't love spending afternoons riding in circles and getting yelled at.

Just love subjecting friends and family to your latest equine video spectacular.

Chiropractor needs a new car.

Wanted to find a place your husband wouldn't go: the barn.

Got tired of spending cold winters by the fire and hot summers by the pool.

Lawyer wanted you to have 3 judges.

Lived for the sport where you could say "piaffe" to the judges.

Had way too much money in bank account.

# A Real Dressage Test

**A:**    Enter extraordinary serpentine.

**X:**    Halt.

**G:**    Try again.

**C:**    Freeze in horror at Judge's stand. Take opportunity to salute hurriedly.

**C:**    Track to left in counter-flexed bolt.

**E:**    Irregular polyhedron left, 20 meters, plus or minus 5 meters.

**FXH:**    Change rein. Unintended jig.

**H:**    Canter, or counter-canter, or cross-canter.

**M-F:**    Working out-of-hand gallop.

**C:**    Down center line, working trot bouncing.

**X:**    Pulley rein. Halt. Salute. Exhale.

Leave arena in free walk, loose language under breath.

# Only Horse People

Know that all topical medications come in either indelible blue or neon Yellow.

Think nothing of eating a sandwich after mucking out stalls.

Believe in the 11th commandment: inside leg to outside rein.

Know why a thermometer has a yard of yarn attached to one end of it.

Are banned from Laundromats.

Fail to associate whips, chains and leather with sexual deviancy.

Can magically lower their voices 5 octaves to bellow at a pawing horse.

Will end relationships over their hobby.

Cluck to their cars to help them up hills.

Insure their horses for more than their cars.

Know more about their horse's nutrition than their own.

Have a vocabulary that can make a sailor blush.

Have a smaller wardrobe than their horse.

Engage in a hobby that is more work than their day job.

Know that mucking stalls is better than Zoloft any day.

# You have a Dressage Rider's Tack Room If:

You own dozens of snaffle bits and they're all exactly alike.

You have so many snaffle bridles that students look disgusted when you say, "Go get the snaffle bridle."

You own every style of bootjack but still need help getting your boots off.

You own the gallon size container of horse treats.

Your last jumping saddle is getting dusty.

You own lots of dressage and lunging whips.

You let everyone borrow anything except your favorite dressage saddle.

You own every size, shape, and color dressage saddle pads come in.

Your favorite girth is the one from the saddle-seat catalog.

You own every style of gel pad available.

Your favorite gloves are falling apart but you can't bear the thought of throwing them out.

You found a mouse nest at the bottom of the pile of unrolled polo wraps.

Your favorite trophy is the plaster cast of your seat from the custom saddle maker.

You favorite blue ribbon is from the show that no longer exists.

# Top 10 Signs Your Dressage Test Needs Some Work

Under judges remarks she writes only: "Nice braid job."

Horse confuses dressage arena rail for a cavaletti; exits at K

Your circles reminds the judge that he should pick up eggs on the way home.

Your serpentine was perfect, except that it was supposed to be a straight centerline.

Sitting trot has caused some fillings to be loosened in lower molars.

Your horse believes "free walk" means leaving the arena and heading towards the nearest patch of grass.

Your working trot had you working harder than your horse.

In your salute your inadvertently use your whip hand causing your horse to perform airs above the ground.

Your walk seems to be more "rare" than "medium."

Impulsion improves only after the horse sees monsters in the decorative shrubbery near letters.

*Emily, age 13.*

# Ten More Signs Your Dressage Test Needs Some Work

---

Your horse's response to the canter aid is "Can't, er, what?"

Your twenty meter circle involved jumping the rail twice.

Your halt took place in the judge's lap, instead of at X.

Your thoroughbred interpreted elasticity to involve trying to kick himself in the head with his back feet during the "working canter".

Your horse entered the arena at A, and M, and H, and B.

Judge's comments include words like "unusual, dramatic, explosive, and tragic."

Leg-yields involve your leg yielding before the horse does.

Free walk was interpreted by your Arab to involve prancing, a rear, and a few bucks.

The judge asks you take the broken letters with you when you leave.

Voodoo dolls of your horse were found in the possession of the show grounds manager.

*Meghan, age 17.*

# The Classical Method of Bucking

Ensure that you have an audience. There is absolutely no point in being decked by your horse unless there are, oh, say a hundred people around to watch. This way, you will have made them feel better about their own inadequacies, and you won't have to go into tedious detail explaining to everyone you know exactly how it happened. It is considered good form if at least one of the audience members is either: Someone you admire and want to impress, someone you despise and don't want to give any ammo to, someone you have the hots for and want to impress, or your best friend, who will have no compunction about falling on the ground, laughing hysterically, and pointing.

Try to be spectacular. I mean, anyone can just get bucked off and land on their backside, can't they? You want to try to make this "the decking to end all deckings."

The Titanic of bucks. You get the picture. Now, for this you will need an extremely acrobatic horse. You want one of those twisty-turny jobbies last seen at the National Rodeo Championships. You also need a supple back. You should practice somersaults, pirouettes and handstands at home.

It is best if this buck happens while everyone is watching you, but no one is prepared for what is to come. During a dressage test is good. Your horse should be working nicely, giving no indication that you are about to become "the person who learned to fly." Of course, experts will point to the tail swishing, the ears twitching back, and the tension around the nostrils, but they are know-it-alls and should be scoffed at. To the uninitiated, this will look like a dramatic performance which you and your horse have practiced at home.

When the horse leaves the ground, and launches you into the air like a cannon ball, it is far more gratifying for the crowd if you can let out a blood-curdling yell. Kind of like William Wallace when they cut his, um, thingies off. Practice this at home. When the local rangers knock on your door, asking if you are keeping a wild cougar in your back yard, you will know you have it right.

You should try to stay elevated as long as possible. The longer, the better. If your arms and legs fly in impossible directions, as if you were a rag doll, you will achieve additional marks for artistic expression.

When you land, try to do so with a thud! The kind of dull thud that you hear when you drop a melon from a great height. Try not to go "splat." It puts the audience off their hamburgers.

Lie immobile for a while, as your horse runs off into the distance. After a suitable time, raise your head and groan, "You b****d".

# Top 10 Exercises for the Equestrian

Drop a heavy steel object on your foot.

Don't pick it up right away. Shout, "get off, Get Off, GET OFF!"

Leap out of a moving vehicle & practice "relaxing into the fall." Roll lithely into a ball and spring to your feet.

Learn to grab your checkbook out of your purse and write out a $200 check without even looking down.

Jog long distances carrying a halter and a carrot. Go ahead and tell the neighbors what you are doing; they might as well know now.

Affix a pair of reins to a moving freight train and practice pulling it to a halt. Smile as if you are having fun!

Hone your fibbing skills: "See, hon', moving hay bales is FUN!" and "No, really, I'm glad your lucky performance and multimillion dollar horse won the blue ribbon. I am just thankful that my hard work and actual ability won me second place."

Practice dialing your chiropractor's number with both arms paralyzed to the shoulder and one foot anchoring the lead rope of a frisky horse.

Borrow the US Army slogan: Be All That You Can Be - bitten, thrown, kicked, slimed, trampled, frozen, etc.

Lie face down in a puddle of mud in your most expensive riding clothes and repeat to yourself: "This is a learning experience, this is a learning experience, this is..."

The number 1 exercise to become a better equestrian—marry money.

# Defining Horses & Riders

## The Riders

**Natural Horseman** looks like a throwback from a Texas ranch, despite the fact that he grew up in Scarsdale, New Jersey. Rope coiled loosely in hand (don't want to send any messages of tension, after all, in case he needs to herd any of those kids on roller blades away from his/her 1-ton dually in the Wal-Mart parking lot. Cowboy hat is strategically placed, and just soiled enough to be cool. Wranglers are well worn, with that little wrinkle above the instep of the ropers, and lots of dust on the lower legs, well, you know, from the round pen.

**Dressage Queen** is freshly coifed. Not even she remembers her true hair color, but she has taken great pains to ensure that Rolfe, the hairdresser, makes the perm and highlights look "natural." Diamond studs are elegant and stately, and not so large that they blind the judge during the entire passage-piaffe tour. $30 denim jumper worn over $300 full seat white breeches and Koenigs.

**Hunter/Jumper** competitor is in an aqua polo and those breeches whose color could be compared to, um, well, okay, let's say they're khaki. The polo is so that folks will think they're a jumper rider until they put on their shirt and stock tie. Baseball cap is mandatory after a ride, in order to provide free advertising to that trainer's stable for whom they shell over a grand or so per month, and to hide "helmet head."

**Eventer** is slightly hunched over. This could be from carrying three saddles, three bridles, three bits, and all related color coordinated gear to every event, or it could possibly be a defensive posture where he/she is unconsciously protecting his/her wallet, which is, of course, nearly empty from buying three saddles, three bridles, three bits and all related color coordinated gear. Looked down on by the H/J's as "people who just run their horses at fences" and by the DQ's as "not real dressage riders." Eventers are smugly convinced that they are in fact the only people in the horse world who CAN ride, since the H/J's don't jump real fences and the DQ's don't ride real horses.

**Endurance Addict** is wearing lycra tights in some neon color. Has not read the rule that lycra is a privilege, not a right. The shinier, the better, so the trail crew can find her body when her mount dumps her down (another) ravine. Wears hiking sneakers of some sort and a smear of trail dirt on the cheek. Sporting one of the zillions of t-shirts she got for paying $75 to complete some other torturous ride. Socks may or may not match (each other).

**Backyard Rider** can be found wearing (in summer) shorts and bra, (in winter) flannel nightgown, muck boots, down jacket. Drives a Ford Tempo filled with dirty blankets and dog hair. Usually has deformed toes on the right foot from being stepped on in the Wal-Mart sneakers that are worn for riding. Roots need touching up to hide the grey. 2-horse bumper-pull behind barn filled with sawdust or hay. Can be found trying to teach her horse to come in the kitchen to eat so she doesn't have to walk all the way to the barn.

# The Horses

**Rusty** is the quintessential NH mount. Rescued from a situation where he was never initiated in the NH ways, he's learned to run down his owners at feeding time, knock children from his back under low hanging branches, and can spit like a camel if provoked. The embezzlement has never been proven. The hospitalization tally for his handlers was twelve until he met Spherical Sam. After twelve minutes in the round pen, he is teaching algebra to high school freshmen, speaks three languages fluently, and can put on his own splint boots (with Spherical Sam's trademark logo clearly embossed).

**Fleistergeidelsprundheim** ("Fleistergeidel" for short) is an 18-hand Warmblood who was bred to make Grand Prix in a European nation where his breeders are still laughing hysterically when they talk about "zat crazy American." Despite being runty, his owner fell in love with his lofty gaits, proud carriage and tremendous athleticism. Never mind that this talent was not revealed until he was chased down by a rabid raccoon, and has not been repeated since. Has been injured 16 times in the last year, preventing his move to PSG at age 6, despite living in a 20' x 20' padded stall and providing family supporting wages to a groom whose chief job duty is "don't let him get hurt!"

**Neverbeenraced** is a prime example of an American Thoroughbred. The coat is deep bay, no markings, the textbook TB head, and no unusual conformational characteristics. Perfect, just perfect. Overcame a near fatal flaw in his H/J career when he learned that the plants in the jumps are NOT real, and therefore did not require him to stop and taste. Has learned to count strides all by himself, and asks in midair which lead his mistress would like today.

**Fastnhighasican** is a Thoroughbred track reject who never won a single race. Perfect eventer! He has two speeds, gallop and stopndump, and they are used, at his discretion, for all three phases of eventing, although he has some creative variations of gallop to spice up that boring dressage test.

There is the gallopdowncenterlineandrear, the gallopdepartandbuck, the extendedoutofhandgallop, and, a favorite among spectators, the gallopzigzagpirouette in which the gallop is performed entirely while hopping on his hind legs. His favorite phase is cross-country where all obstacles regardless of size are jumped at the height of 5.5 feet, and because that is where he gets to employ his personal favorite movement, the stopndump. This is the most fun when performed at cross-country water obstacles where his person invariably stands up soaking wet with murky, smelly water and threatens to sell him to Fleistergeidel's owner while he follows up with another fun gallop variation, the imfreeandyoucantcatchmegallop, another crowd-pleaser.

**Al Kamar Raka Shazaam** is an Arabian horse who was often called "you bastard" by his former owner until he found his current owner—as hyper as he—an endurance addict. Can spook at a blowing leaf, spin a 360 and not lose his big trot rhythm or give up an inch to the horse behind him. Has learned to eat, drink, pee and drop to his resting pulse rate on command. Has compiled 3,450 AERC miles, with his rider compiling 3,445. Those five miles being the ones he was chased down the trail after performing his trademark 360 turn, without aforementioned rider.

**Snook'ums** is the backyard rider's horse. Big head; stride of a gerbil. Duct tape holding shoe on until farrier gets out next month. Has a little Quarter, Arab, Standardbred, Tennessee Walker, Shetland blood. Mane cut with scissors straight across. He's been there so long she forgot how she got him or where he came from. Frequently seen ambling around the yard. Been known to join family picnics on the back porch.

# Frequently Overheard

**NH Devotee:** "Well, shucks ma'am, tweren't nuthin'! It's simple horsemanship. With this special twirly flickitat'em rope ($17.95 plus tax), you'll be round-penning like me in no time."

**Dressage Queen**: "Oh no, he's hurt again? The check is in the mail." To Herr Germanlastname: "Can't you tune up those one tempis for me?" To the groom: "Get me that mounting block. Can't you see my nails are still wet?" To the show manager: "That footing has ruined my chances at Olympic Gold in 2012, I'll have you know. And what were you thinking, stabling me next to that nobody? That horse could be diseased!" To anyone who will listen: "When I had dinner with Hilda / Lendon / Robert…"

**H/J Competitor**: "Did you tell Neverbeenraced how many strides between fence four and fence five? I can never remember! Is my butt sticking out enough when I post? Oh no, I can't jump 2'6, my trainer will KILL me! I can't wait to do jumpers with Neverbeenraced. Then we can wear one of those tasseled ear covers!"

**Eventer**: "I broke my collarbone/ribs/ankle again last week, but I'll be fine for the jog-up tomorrow. How do you get pond water out of saddle leather? Did you see our show jumping where Fastnhighasican bounced the two stride combination? Did you see our final gallopdowncenterlineandrear? I think he is finally starting to relax in dressage. Oh, it's just a little concussion. Have you seen my horse?"

**Endurance Addict**: "Anyone have Advil? Anyone have food? I think last year's Twinkies finally went bad. For this pain, I spend money? Oh, I never bring hay or water to the vet checks, there's always plenty around. Quick, quick, did you look, was his pee okay? Shazaam, you bastard! It's just a leaf!" [thud]

**Backyard Rider**: "It's too hot/cold/wet/dry to ride. I used to show. Where's my Metamucil? Has anyone seen Snook'ums? Last I saw he was across the road in the cornfield. Here's a picture of Snook'ums when he was 43 years young! Snook'ums stop slobbering on me."

# A Horse's View of Natural Horsemanship

Hello my name is Flicka and my Owner's a clinic junky. Yes, it's true. She went through her mid-life crisis, came to the sale barn, and bought me.

I spent my whole life misbehaving and being passed from greenhorn to greenhorn until someone finally got smart and sent me to the sale barn.

I was seriously hoping to be picked up by one of those show horse fellas so I could live in a fancy barn and stand around all day looking pretty, but they told me my butt's too small, my heads too big, and the crest on my neck from a bout with grass founder (thanks to owner number 2) is not desirable, and in general I was just not that capable of looking pretty. So I went home with Phyllis instead.

She pets me and loves me. In general I had a pretty good life at first. Then she heard about those guys who whisper to horses. Life has never been the same.

First there was Pat. At Pat's clinic Phyllis learned to twirl a big stick and chase me around a round pen till I was ringing wet with sweat.

Once I had "calmed down" (I was never really fired up in the first place until that guy came at me like an idiot with the stick) she began learning to ride me with no bridle. Talk about giving an old spoiled horse an opportunity to have some fun! Initially I went along with it. I'd lope around the pen real nice like, and everyone would oooh and ahhh over my "natural horse" abilities.

Then, just when everyone had gathered around to watch, I would see the SCARIEST!! (tehehehe) shadow in the history of scary shadows, switch directions, and take off with my rider clinging terrified to my back. Every other horse on the place was envious of me because their owners would take them out back and beat them with that overpriced stick when no one was watching, but I knew my Phyllis would not.

Eventually Philly (as I like to call her) gave up on the whole natural horse idea when Pat tried to talk her into jumping me without a bridle over some barrels.

Off we went in search of another guru. In our search we found Monty. He threw a string at a horse and talked to the horse with winks and stares. I spent some time with his clinic horses. I saw the demonstration where an unbroken 2 year old became an overnight reiner.

Later I talked to the 2 year old. He was actually 5 and had been doing this same routine for the entire tour. The first time Phyllis broke out the string, I again, went along with it. Well, until she got tired of me stopping and looking at her like she was stupid. When she went to get herself a bottle of water and refer to that chapter in Monty's book, I grabbed the string and chewed it to pieces.

Then there was the Indian fella with a name I can't pronounce. To get the full effect of his clinic Philly painted stuff on my body and put feathers in my hair. I looked like I was in a costume class. But hey whatever floats your boat. I thought maybe at least with this guy we might get to play Indian pony games and have mock battles or something but no. More round pen work and gimmicks. This time there was a fire in the middle of the round pen and they danced around it while praying that I would become a good horse and always mind my owner. He only took her for a couple thousand pelts and a bottle of firewater.

There's been the Australian guy. Training with a boomerang while he hopped around like a kangaroo and called me his mate... "Sorry fella, you're cute and all, but my mate has 4 legs. I just don't swing interspecies."

A horse psychic who told Phyllis my momma didn't lick me enough when I was born.

A guy who used his hands like ears to talk to me and of course the touchy-feely lady.

I can't complain though I've got an owner who loves me and has devoted her time to trying to make me a better horse. I really should behave, really I should, but I think I am contributing to her youth by giving her a reason to take me to all these clinics. Maybe the next clinic will involve turning me out with the mustangs so I find my inner wild stallion.

Sincerely, Flicka

# Ariel The New Age Trainer

Riding high on the success of such books as *You're My Mare Not My Mother* and *Denial Ain't What Keeps The Horseshoe On*, Ariel is holding clinics across the country to promote her latest book and infomercials *From A Whisper To A Scream: When Your Horse Can't Hear You.*

The plucky blonde, so progressive in her methods of equine communication she's called *The Woman Who E-Mails Horses*, is the first woman to receive national attention in the growing field of touchy-feely horse training.

Although successful, Ariel has been criticized for her unorthodox techniques and is the first to admit she's not a traditional horse trainer.

"Training is such a worn out concept, even the word 'train' is archaic, it comes from the Old French *trahiner*, to drag. And that's just what training is, a BIG DRAG!

"What I'm interested in is communicating with problem horses, letting them know they're not alone. Since I too have issues with trust and a history of abusive, dysfunctional relationships, I understand what they're going through. I can also relate to frustrated riders. As I wrote in *You're My Mare Not My Mother*, at one point a guilt-tripping gelding shamed me into believing if I were a prettier, thinner, smarter person I wouldn't be having riding problems.

"My goal is to facilitate people away from the 'Self-Centered' riding made popular in the 1980s to a more 'Co-Dependent' riding where the horse and rider work closely to deepen their relationship and become enmeshed in the riding experience."

In defense of reports that her clinics are among the most expensive in this new industry, Ariel is unapologetic. "You get what you pay for. Horses are individuals and it takes time to discover what form of communication works best for them. Whispering to horses is fine, but some respond better to murmuring or babbling, while still others prefer mime or slide shows. I have found when working with a herd, semaphore is the most effective."

Ariel further points out that not all bad horse behavior is the result of a negative breaking experience. "Horses are very sensitive and can have a variety of problems, both emotional and paranormal. They can suffer from depression, low self-esteem, eating disorders, even repressed memories. Most people are unaware of the large number of horses who are survivors of alien abduction. I have found that repressed memories of such abductions are the primary cause of trailering difficulties. There are also horses unfairly labeled 'spooky,' when their behavior is actually an appropriate response to poltergeist activity."

Ariel's symposiums cover a wide range of topics, such as: Reimprinting the Inner Foal, Obsessive/Compulsive Dressage, Gymkhanta, Andalusians of Grandeur, Bi-Polar Bending, A.D.D. in Arabians, Fear of Flying Lead Changes, and Feeling Suicidal? Consider Eventing.

When not on tour, Ariel offers weekend retreats at Passing Wind, her Malibu, California Ranch, that focus on specific breeds and riding disciplines. She will also customize sessions to meet a client's particular needs and budget.

"Once we even re-birthed a Tennessee Walker to help her face her 'water issues.' It was exhilarating and only 3 or 4 people were injured." Ariel was unable to comment further on this event as the matter is still in litigation.

Ariel began developing her techniques under the tutelage of GoWaan-PoOLmiFynGer, the charismatic shaman of the Diamond-Phillips tribe and author of the ground breaking book, *Horse Buck Hard*.

"The whole monosyllabism of Horse Buck Hard overwhelmed me with its Zen. I knew instantly I had to study with him."

GoWaanPoOLmiFynGer introduced Ariel to his tribe's ancient practices of Equine-Aromatherapy, Prance-Channeling, Stall Feng Shui, Public Relations, and Marketing.

"GoWaan taught me so much. Not only did I learn how frequently riders with dysfunctional personal lives project unresolved emotional issues onto their horses, but the outrageous amounts of money they are willing to pay to be told it isn't their fault."

Ariel went on to become GoWaanPoOLmiFynGer's assistant when he toured to promote his calendar and video, Buckskin, Beads, and Beefcake. "It was a great gig," she reflects, "but I knew it wouldn't last, when I noticed most of the women attending his sold-out clinics didn't have horses."

She next traveled to the Australian outback, where she studied with acclaimed Snowy River Kanguru Bruce Fosters, whose masterwork, *The Principles of Bonding-From Brumbies to The Boardroom*, has become an integral part of the executive training programs of many multinational corporations. "Bruce is an incredible visionary. He was the first person to theorize that a rearing horse is really just asking for a hug!"

Since starting her own clinics, Ariel has emphasized the differences between her methods and those of her contemporaries, but she does admit to performing the crowd pleasing, ubiquitous get an unstarted horse to accept a saddle, bit, bridle and rider without breaking its spirit in under an hour demonstration.

"Of course, since I'm using the techniques I've developed, my version is different from what people have come to expect after seeing other clinicians. For example, I find using a pyramid-shaped pen, instead of a round pen, brings more energy to the session. I also use indirect lighting, scented candles and soft music. I start by having a few glasses of wine with the horse, and then begin to recount my earliest childhood memories of separation and abandonment, while lunging the horse at a trot. After several minutes of this, usually at the point in my litany of victimization where my abusive second husband leaves me for my farrier, the horse will begin to go through a visible change. While still at a trot, it will start shaking its head and trying to cover its ears. This is the moment I call 'The Throw Up.' The Throw Up is the point a horse reaches when it can't stand listening to my problems anymore and will do anything to get me to stop, including being saddled, bridled and ridden for the first time. People think it's magic when they see how willing the horse becomes once I shut up and start saddling, but there's nothing mysterious about it. I just have a very annoying voice and more issues than *TV Guide*."

Future goals for Ariel include developing a web site, and a 900 number. "I envision a network where for only 3.99 per minute, riders can speak to their own Psychic Tele-Trainer, who I've personally educated. I also plan to explore the financial aspects of communicating with other animal species. I'm willing to discourse with dogs or chat with cats. I'll even vocalize with vermin if there's money in it."

# Political Correctness & The Horse Community

The horse world is dreadfully guilty of political incorrectness. Citizens, we can fix this!

From now on, the rider who came in 128th out of 127 competitors isn't a major loser; he's ribbon-deprived.

We'll refer to awful jumpers as potential dressage horses and horrid dressage horses will be called event prospects (oh, wait, we've been doing that for years anyway).

Prominent horse people who go to jail for tax evasion are, um, ethically challenged.

Judges who make stupid decisions are myopically magnificent.

A twitch is a lip tourniquet.

Instructors, refrain from telling a student that she has a bad seat. Instead, tell this rider that she has astronomical potential for butt improvement.

A horse that always crashes through the jumps is merely in touch with his personal sense of gravity. Likewise, a bad mover isn't an eggbeater with legs, he's kinetically challenged.

A horse who won't go forward is a whoa-overachiever.

Waterlogged show grounds are humidity enriched.

The real problem is that the term 'politically incorrect' is politically incorrect. It's too critical. The whole point is to single out someone's most sensitive trouble area and then simultaneously glorify the fortitude it takes to overcome the matter while completely avoiding any clear reference to the actual problem. Hey, we're truth-impaired, but we're sensitive! A better term for politically incorrect would be "socially under-euphemized."

Like the political correctness craze, the trend toward *uber*-safety has affected the equestrian world. Riders are advised to sleep with their helmets on. Horses who routinely buck their riders off should also wear certified helmets just in case a falling equestrian impacts at a high rate of speed with an equine noggin. In fact, goggles might a good idea for horses that buck: riders are just full of sharp edges like fingernails and elbows and a poke in the eye can be quite painful.

In an attempt to promote better safety for horses and riders, here are some new warning labels to consider:

Do not place hay net over head while skydiving or eating corn on the cob.

Warning: insect repellent may infringe upon the constitutional rights of the insect community. Consult attorney before spraying.

Please remove riding breeches before placing in dryer.

When saddle-breaking three-year-old horses, apply leg sparingly. If swelling or redness of rider occurs, discontinue immediately and seek professional trainer.

Warning! Surface of arena is closer than it appears. Much, much closer.

Inflate ponies to 50 psi when cold.

Do not affix jumper cables to your big toes when engine is on. (This has nothing to do with horses. It's just plain good advice.)

# A Horse Show in Heaven

One day in Heaven, Saint Peter, Saint Paul, and Saint John were standing around near the horse paddocks, bored, watching the horses frolic.

"I know!" Peter exclaimed. "Why don't we have a horse show?"

"Who are we going to compete against, Peter?" Paul asked.

The trio pondered this a moment when Peter said, "We'll invite Satan. I mean, all of the World and National Champion horses are here in heaven. His stable is filled with the spoiled, difficult, and mean critters. We're certain to win."

And so they called Satan and invited him to their horse show. Satan asked why they would want to be humiliated like that, because he would certainly beat them.

Peter, Paul, and John didn't understand. Incredulous, Peter asked, "We have all of the champion horses up here in heaven! How could you possibly beat us?"

Satan laughed and replied, "Have you forgotten, gentlemen? I have all the judges."

# The Right Way to Mount a Horse

Mounting a horse is actually very easy if it is done properly. A rider can only mount a horse from one side because a horse only likes to be mounted from one side. The left side is right and the right side is wrong. You're right to be left and wrong to be right. If you mount from the front, you mount from the right, which is then the left because your right is its left, and the left the right, keeping in mind that the left is right and the right is wrong. Put your left to your right and step so your right is to the wrong and now your right is opposite its left and left the right. To right right is to the left and to right is wrong is to the right, but backwards, the right is right and the left is wrong only when your right is on its wrong, and the left is on its right. Switching right to left and left to right is wrong. Right is wrong and left is right only from the front or else the left is right and the right is wrong.

# Murphy's Horse Laws

There is no such thing as a sterile barn cat.

No one ever notices how you ride until you fall off.

A horse's misbehavior will be in direct proportion to the number of people who are watching.

The least useful horse in you barn will eat the most, require shoes twice as often as any other horse in the barn, and a vet call every four weeks.

If you're wondering if you left the water on in the barn, you did. If you're wondering if you latched the pasture gate, you didn't.

If you approach within fifty feet of your barn in clean clothes, you will get dirty.

The number of horses you own will increase to the number of stalls in your barn.

Hoof picks migrate.

If you fall off, you will land on the site of your most recent injury.

An uncomplicated horse can be ruined with enough schooling.

You can't push a horse on a lunge line.

If you are winning, quit. There is only one way to go. Down!

If you do a thorough check of your trailer before hauling, your truck will break down.

Clipper blades will become dull only when the horse is half finished. Clipper motors will quit only when you have the horse's head left to trim.

One horse isn't enough; two is too many.

If a horse is advertised as "under $5000" you can bet he isn't $1500.

You can't run a barn without bailing twine.

Wind velocity increases in proportion to how well your hat fits.

There is no such thing as the right feed.

Your favorite tack always gets chewed on, and your new blanket gets torn.

Tack you hate never wears out; blankets you hate cannot be destroyed; horses you hate cannot be sold and will outlive you.

Never lick a gift horse in the mouth.

# Changing the Light Bulb

## Horses

**Warmblood:** Light bulb? What light bulb?

**Haflinger:** Show me where it is and I'll do it, no problem! Can I clean a little too while I'm at it? You want me to fix lunch for you to while I'm at it?

**Any foal:** The sun is shining, the day is young. We've got our whole lives ahead of us and you're inside worrying about a stupid burned-out light bulb?

**Thoroughbred:** Just one. And he'll rewire the barn while he's at it.

**Shetland pony:** I can't reach the stupid lamp.

**Saddlebred:** Sorry, just had my hooves and mane done.

**Morgan:** Oh, oh, me, me! Pleeeze let me change the light bulb!

**Quarter Horse:** Let him do it, you can pet me while he's busy.

**Trakhener:** Light bulb? Light bulb? That thing I just ate was a light bulb?

**Akhal-Teke:** Zero! AT's aren't afraid of the dark!

**Holsteiner:** How DARE that light bulb burn out! How DARE you ask me to change it! OH, the nerve! (Flouncing off)

**Appaloosa:** No, don't change it. If it's dark, maybe no one will see me raiding the feed room.

**Arab:** That's what we pay the help for. I'll just chew on his shirttail while he's at it.

**Connemara:** We'll just be after havin' a nip of the Bushmill's, we will, and then we'll not be noticin' the light.

**Andalusian:** Let the maid do it. I need to go roll in the mud.

**Clydesdale:** Och, and ye'll just be usin' up the 'lectricity, ye' will, better tae use a wee bit of candle...better yet tae not waste either and just gae tae sleep when the sun gaes doon. Electiricity is verra dear.

**National Show Horse:** (fidgeting all the while): Lights? Lights? Where? Do you want me to pose? This is my good side...no, wait, let me get my mane straight...no wait, this angle is all wrong. No, wait, maybe this is my good side. Do you want dramatic..or bold..or maybe sensitive...?

**Shire:** (Yawn) Who cares?

**Cob:** Just wait till I've finished my hay net before you even consider asking me to do anything. Can't you see I'm busy?

# Riders

**Western Pleasure Rider:** Oh, my God, someone fix that bulb, I have to have light so that my silver and spangles all sparkle and glow their best and so that all the highlighter on Old Peanut Head makes his nose look so smooth and sparkly, and oh, my diamond studs have to flash in the light, you know, so oh, someone has to fix it, oh, maybe you without all the silver on your saddle, obviously you can't ride, you can do it.

**Endurance Rider:** Light bulb? Do you mind, I'm trying to get my horse's pulse/respiration/hydration levels to acceptable levels. Once that's done, I have another 50 miles to go before I can even think about changing a light bulb.

**Dressage Queen:** Change a light bulb? Are you joking? I couldn't possibly be expected to subject myself to such a menial task. Change it yourself. Oh, and wash your hands when you are finished. The very thought!

**Classical Dressage Queen:** These things cannot be rushed, but must be approached slowly, with great patience, and adherence to the principles laid down by the classical masters, otherwise the light bulb will not attain its true potential, but will forever just be a shadow of its true self. Never, ever, use any type of gadget when changing the light bulb. That is an offense to the principles of classical light bulb changing.

**Eventer:** As soon as my arm is out of this sling, broken after falling off at that large stone wall while riding Hell Bent for Leather cross-country, I'll change it. Until then, deal with the dark. It'll put hair on your chest. Only dressage riders require lights, anyway.

**Show Jumper:** Why on Earth would I need to change a light bulb when the whole world knows that the sun shines out of my ass. Why, when I release over a jump, the spectators are practically blinded.

**Natural Horseman:** You must instill respect in the light bulb, so that it sees you as the Alpha light bulb, using "light bulb dynamics" (video set available at $179.00 on my Website). Once you have done this, you will find that there is really no need to change the light bulb at all, but that the light bulb will, with very little coaxing from you (using patented "light bulb coaxer" designed by me–$99.00 each, for an extra $49.99 you get an introductory video thrown in) behave as all good light bulbs should.

**Hunter Rider:** Well, I'm waiting for my trainer to tell me exactly how. But he's changing light bulbs somewhere else right now.

**Sidesaddle Rider:** Well, one thing's for certain: if they can do it, I can do it, and with both legs on the same side of the step ladder. Stand back and watch me! But first I have to find my top hat and veil, cut the crusts off the sandwich and pack it in a linen napkin, fold my rain gloves with the thumbs together and place them under the billets, have my saddle re-stuffed and make an apron.

**Fox Hunter:** If you laid out all your kit the night before the hunt, you wouldn't need to worry about the light bulb. You'd be on your way. Forget the light bulb. Ain't got no time to worry 'bout no light bulb. HOUNDS ARE RUNNING! Load in the dark ( in August), unload in the dark (in December) - what's the big deal? (But please don't forget that flask and Snickers bar!)

# High School Cliques

**Quarter Horses:** Definitely jocks. Strutting around flexing those muscles, showing off their butts. Definitely jocks.

**Thoroughbreds:** Preppies. Sometime athletes, never "jocks." Monogrammed blankets, leather halters, Nike eventer shoes, the latest custom trailer and tack. They are the "new money" rich.

**Appaloosas:** Could only be the stoners. They like to trip acid so they can watch their spots move.

**Arabians:** RAH! RAH! SIS BOOM BAH! GOOOOOOOOOOOOOOOOOOOOO TEAM! (need I say more?)

**Shetland Ponies:** Frightening, spiky hairdos, snotty attitudes, and any color of the rainbow. Gotta be PUNKS. Some even sport tattoos.

**Friesians:** Big, buff, and always in black, they are the biker clique. Cigarettes hanging out of the corners of their mouths, dangerous glint in the eyes, daring anyone to cross their path.

**Morgans:** They're the nerdy teacher's pets, running around doing everything from yearbook to decorating the gym and ratting out the bikers, stoners, and jocks. They have perpetual wedgies.

**Drafts:** (all breeds) No real clique, they're just the big guys who sit in the back of the room and fart (a lot). And then laugh. Who's going to STOP them?

**Icelandics and Paso Finos:** They're the little squirrely geeks who flit around a dance trying to fit in and fail miserably. The kind who wear Toughskins jeans from Sears (or would that be rip-off WeathaBeetas?).

**Akhal-Tekes:** Foreign exchange students. And no one else can spell their names either.

**Hackney Ponies:** A breed this manic would have to be a band geek. Marching along with their knees and heads held high.....even when going to the bathroom.

**Warmbloods:** Old Money Preppies, as opposed to the TBs who are new money preppies. All their tack is imported from Europe, they drink Perrier water and eat only organically-grown feed. They look down on everyone and talk amongst themselves about summer in Paris and skiing in Gstad and wasn't it dreadful how provincial Spruce Meadows has become?

# Opening the Gate

---

**Lipizzaner:** No need for opening it! When are you all going to learn how to fly?

**Thoroughbred:** I don't want to mess with that gate and I am too scared of flying! I'll just jump over it and leave you all behind.

**Paint:** Yeah, what he said! Na Na Na Na Na Na!

**Palomino:** Forget it. Count me out. I'm not taking any chances of messing up my chrome!

**Arabian:** You'll have to get somebody else to do it. I'm not messin' up my nails for anyone!

**Quarter Horse:** Maybe if I push on it with my big buns, I could open it!

**Standardbred:** Pity on all of you. I'll figure it out, just give me some time.

**Polo Pony:** Wait just a minute, let me get my stick and give it a few bloody whacks!

**Shetland:** Let me at it. I'll break the stupid thing! Then you all can get out of my face.

**Mule:** Oh, let's just pack it in and call it a day.

**Saddlebred:** Now, now. I'll open it, if someone could help me with my shoes?

**Friesian:** I'll do it! Do you think it will mess up my hair? I always have such good hair days.

**Mustang:** Heck with opening it, how about I just run the whole darn fence over?

**Belgian:** Step back! You all aren't strong enough to do it. I'll do it. Oh, but what if I break it?

**Morgan:** There, there. I'll do it for you. No need to have such a big fit. Peace be with all of you. Is there anything else I could do for you after I get done with the gate?

**Appaloosa:** Oh, hush all of you! Ya big bunch of sissies. No one is leaving until I say so!

**Percheron:** I opened the gate while you've been arguing! I even went down the next row and opened all the other gates. So it will be awhile before I have to listen to you argue again!

# Horse Health Care

---

"You have to help me, Doc. My horse is starting to believe he's a pretzel."

"Well, I'll see if I can straighten him out."

"Doc, my horse thinks he's a bullfrog."

"Hmmm, how long has this thing been going on?"

"Ever since he was a little tadpole."

"Doctor, my horse thinks he's a ten-dollar bill."

"Go shopping. You need the change."

"Doctor, can you help my horse out?"

"Certainly, which way did he come in?"

Vet: "What's wrong with your horse?"

Owner: "He thinks he's a chicken."

Vet: "How long has this been going on?"

Owner: "Oh, about 6 months."

Vet: "6 months? Why didn't you bring him in sooner?"

Owner: "Because we needed the eggs!"

"Did you hear about the vet surgeon who cut off the horse's left side by mistake?"

"No, I didn't. How's the horse?"

"Oh, he's all right now."

Owner: "Doctor, my horse is acting funny today. What should I do?"

Vet: "Try open mic night at a comedy club."

The owner of a dude ranch boasted that he had the best horse in the world.

"I was riding him through the woods one day when he stumbled over a rock. I fell from the saddle and broke my leg. We were miles from the ranch and even further from civilization."

"Don't tell me," the city visitor said, "that the horse reset your leg, and nursed you back to health out in the wilderness. Then carried you back to the ranch."

"No, but he grabbed me be the belt, dragged me home, and called a doctor."

"I'm glad everything turned out so well." said the visitor.

"Not really. He called a veterinarian."

"Doctor, my horse thinks it's a bird."

"Have it perch over there and I'll tweet it in a moment."

"How is the horse who swallowed the half dollar?"

"No change yet."

On Timmy's birthday, his parents bought him what he always wanted: a race horse. But the horse didn't seem to be in very good shape. So Timmy took it to the vet.

"This is a very old horse," the vet said.

"Will I be able to race him?" asked Timmy.

The vet looked at Timmy and then he looked at the horse. "Sure," he said, "and you'll probably win."

"Doctor, will this ointment cure my horse's spots?"

"I never make rash judgments."

"Doctor, my horse swallowed my pen! What should I do?"

"Use a pencil until I get there."

"Doctor, my horse swallowed a roll of film."

"Let's hope nothing develops."

"How is your health these days?"

"I sleep soundly and eat like a horse."

"Let's leave your table manners out of this."

A patient had an automobile phobia, and his psychiatrist (a bit old-fashioned) said, "If you had a horse you wouldn't have to drive a car.

"But, Doc," he protested, "Horses can't drive cars!"

"Please, Doc. I can't ride my horse any more. I think I'm a needle!"

"Hmmmm. I see your point!"


"Help me doctor, I'm not well."

"What seems to be the trouble ?"

"Well I work like a horse, I eat like a bird, and I'm as tired as a dog. "

"Sounds like you ought to see a veterinarian, not a doctor."


Owner: "How much would you charge for pulling my horse's tooth?"

Vet: "$90."

Owner: "What? $90 for just a few minutes work?"

Vet: "I can do it slower if you like."


A woman went to a psychiatrist and said she was in great distress over her husband.

"He thinks he's a horse. He sleeps standing up and he neighs instead of speaking. He even insists on being fed oats in a bag." said the woman "It's terrible! "

"How long has this been going on?" asked the doctor.

"Six, maybe eight months." she replied.

"You have let things go too far," said the doctor. "Your husband will require a great deal of very expensive treatment.

"I don't care about the expense," said the wife. "I'll pay you anything! Anything at all to make my husband stop thinking he's a horse."

"But it will cost many thousands of dollars, can you afford this level of treatment?" asked the doctor.

"Why of course we can," said the woman. "He's already won three races this season at Aqueduct."

# Living with Obsessive Compulsive Equine Attachment Neurosis Syndrome (OCEANS)

Just recently, after years of research, I have finally been able to give a name to what my wife and I have been living with for years.

It's an affliction, for sure, which when undiagnosed and misunderstood can devastate and literally tear a family apart. Very little is known about OCEANS. But it is my hope this article will generate interest from researchers involved in the equine and psychological sciences. You will, no doubt, begin to identify similar symptoms in your own family and hopefully, with this information, be able to cope.

OCEANS is usually found in the female and can manifest itself anytime from birth to the golden years. Symptoms may appear any time and may even go dormant in the late teens, but the syndrome frequently re-emerges in later years.

Symptoms vary widely in both number and degree of severity. Allow me to share some examples which are most prominent in our home.

## The afflicted individual:

Can smell moldy hay at ten paces, but can't tell whether milk has gone bad until it turns chunky.

Finds the occasional "Buck and toot" session hugely entertaining, but severely chastises her husband for similar antics.

Will spend hours cleaning and conditioning her tack, but wants to eat on paper plates so there are no dishes.

Considers equine gaseous emissions a fragrance.

Enjoys mucking out four stalls twice a day, but insists on having a housekeeper mop the kitchen floor once a week.

Will spend an hour combing and trimming an equine mane, but wears a baseball cap so she doesn't waste time brushing her own hair.

Will dig through manure piles daily looking for worms, but does not fish.

Will not hesitate to administer a rectal exam up to her shoulder, but finds cleaning out the Thanksgiving turkey cavity for dressing quite repulsive.

By memory can mix eight different supplements in the correct proportions, but can't make macaroni and cheese that isn't soupy.

Twice a week will spend an hour scrubbing algae from the water tanks, but has a problem cleaning lasagna out of the casserole dish.

Will pick a horse's nose, and call it cleaning, but becomes verbally violent when her husband picks his.

Can sit through a four-hour session of a ground work clinic, but unable to make it through a half-hour episode of Cops.

## The spouse of the OCEANS afflicted individual:

Must come to terms with the fact there is no cure, and only slightly effective treatments. The syndrome may be genetic or caused by the inhaling of manure particles which, I propose, have an adverse effect on female hormones.

Must adjust the family budget to include equine items: Hay, veterinarian, farrier, riding boots and clothes, supplements, tack, equine masseuse, acupuncturist. As well as the (mandatory) equine spiritual guide. Once you have identified a monthly figure, never look at it again. Doing so will cause tightness in your chest, nausea, and occasional diarrhea.

Must realize that your spouse has no control over this affliction. More often than not, she will deny a problem even exists as denial is common.

Must form a support group. You need to know you're not alone and there's no shame in admitting your wife has a problem. My support group, for instance, includes men who enjoy motorcycling, four-day weekends around a camp fire telling tall tales, and drinking lots of scotch. Skiing, snowmobiling, hunting, fishing. Most times, she is unaware that I am even gone, until the precise moment she needs help getting a 50-pound bag of grain out of the truck.

Now you can better see how OCEANS affects countless households in this country and abroad. It knows no racial, ethnic or religious boundaries. It is a syndrome that will be difficult to treat because those most affected are in denial and therefore, not interested in a cure.

So, I am taking it upon myself to be constantly diligent in my research in order to pass along information to make it easier for caretakers to cope on a day to day basis.

*Scooter Grubb*

# Things Not to Say to Your Farrier

---

That's not the way they did it on that horseshoeing show.

You sure earned your money on that one!

If you just give each of the dogs a piece of hoof they'll get out from under the horse and quit fighting.

If he didn't kick like that, I'd trim him myself.

My weanling colt needs a trim, and I figured you could halter break him at the same time.

Can we shoe him in the arena? When he rears in the barn, he hits his head.

I read all about the "Natural Way" to trim on the internet, and you're supposed to...

Good morning glad you're here can we reschedule? I have a lot going on today.

Can you shoe him so that he doesn't paw?

Most times when he kicks, he misses!

Just do the hinds I'll do the fronts.

I'm sure glad you don't mind working on muddy feet.

I got a bargain on these shoes at a rummage sale, could you use them instead and save me some money?

I've got a new horse whose feet are in pretty bad shape. The previous owners said their farrier wouldn't work on him.

I know it's been a long day for you; that's why I saved the worst one for last.

I don't understand why the shoes didn't stay on. I just had them done 12 weeks ago.

He won't stand for me either, but your ad said you were a professional.

Yep, I put that stuff on their feet right before you got here.

Isn't it great to be outside all day?

It sure is HOT!

I used to shoe, and I can tell right away if you're doing a good job.

Honestly, I DO clean his feet.

I haven't ever picked up his feet, but he seems real gentle.

Can you put these shoes on good and tight so that they won't come off?

He's never been that bad! What did you do?

I left them out in the field because it was such a nice day.

Since he's a colt, will you charge me half price?

I used to shoe my own horses, but I could never get the angles right.

Do you think you could take a little more off that back foot?

That's not the way the farrier did it back where I come from.

Boy, you must have a strong back to bend over all day like that.

# Ancient Wisdom

---

*Dakota tribal wisdom says that when you discover you're riding a dead horse, the best strategy is to dismount. However in the business world we usually brainstorm potential solutions. Case in point:*

Business dashboard red-flags customer shipping schedule slowdown.

Data drill-down identifies performance slippage in on-shore production facility.

The associate in charge of horses indicates that performance slippage was noted in enterprise-wide knowledge base.

Production analyst team generated Ishikawa diagram to identify the root cause source of variation.

Blamestorming ensues. Management smart-sizes associate for failure to utilize open-door face-time opportunities with C-level offices to identify short- and long-term strategic gaps, and synergize nimble, future-proof alternatives.

Multidisciplinary task force is empowered to re-engineer business processes to incorporate six sigma total-quality driven, client-facing team dynamics.

Senior management visits similar organizations to identify best-of-breed practices for addressing dead horse productivity issues. Meeting planner schedules four-star hotels and resorts to provide optimal environment for networking and frank discussion.

Appoint a cluster team to study the organizational experience slippage that led to dead horse chain of events.

Cluster team conceptualizes vision and mission statements for dead horse.

Finance department authorizes dead horse buy vs. build analysis to optimize ROI. Potential off-shore partnerships identified.

Deputy CFO authorizes flex-time for living-impaired horse to improve morale.

Human resources demands that the dead horse must be reclassified as "living-impaired" in order to meet EEOC guidelines. Schedule all-hands living-impaired horse awareness training seminar. Incorporate role-playing scenarios.

HR recommends performance incentives for living-impaired horse to improve environmental accountability.

HR engages life coach to act as change catalyst enabling living-impaired horse to incorporate lessons learned.

Rider identified as key stakeholder. Performance goals updated to include effective change management skills to manage living-impaired horse productivity.

Tiger team architects knowledge base of repeatable processes for riding living-impaired horse.

Send the living-impaired horse and rider to a team-dynamics retreat.

Apply for federal grant to study how the living-impaired horse can contribute to the green economy. Apply for carbon offsets. Request additional funding to implement bleeding-edge, future-proof seminar series.

Commission a productivity study to determine if a lighter rider improves the living-impaired horse's performance.

Harness two living-impaired horses together to double performance.

Declare that the living-impaired horse is "better, faster, and cheaper."

Declare that the living-impaired horse was procured with cost as an independent variable.

Declare that since it has been determined that the living-impaired horse does not have to be fed, it is cash-neutral.

Ride the living-impaired horse "smarter not harder."

Ride the living-impaired horse "outside the box."

Grab "low hanging fruit" while riding living-impaired horse.

Name the living-impaired horse "Paradigm Shift" and keep riding it.

Form a quality circle to identify other uses for living-impaired horse.

Repurpose living-impaired horse to improve return on investment.

At end of the day, promote the living-impaired horse to a supervisory position.

# You Know You are a Horse Person When

---

## Office Environment

You show up at work with bran mash all over the back of your coat.

Your secretary does a "hay check" on your suit each morning and your first stop in the office is the ladies room to remove the shavings from your shoes.

You don't notice the barn smells on your clothes/shoes and wonder why "regular" folks are sniffing the air.

All of your clothes have horsehair on them, even if they've never been worn to the barn.

You pull change from your pocket at work. Alfalfa, shavings, and braiding bands fall out onto the floor.

Co-workers start pointing out green slobber or straw on your clothes. Your solution is to start wearing hunter green exclusively.

You show up in city clothes dressed for appointments and when you get there people reach over the breakfast table to pick alfalfa out of your hair.

You are walking up the stairs to your office and you see a patch of mud on the stairs. On closer observation, it appears to have bits of hay and manure in it. You stop, look around to make sure nobody is around, and you pick it up and drop it to the very bottom of the stairwell where nobody ever goes. Because you just know it came from YOUR boots.

You are in a meeting, and you say something in Command Voice, and someone asks you, "Do you train dogs, or something?"

Your fellow office workers (all male) ask you to swap out the empty water bottle for a full one. They know darn well that you are only one who can lift a five gallon water bottle (weighing in at a good 40 pounds or so) over your head AND aim it properly at the dispenser without spilling a drop! And you thought lugging those sacks of horse feed and emptying them into 55 gallon feed drums didn't have any side benefits?

Your car is the only one in the company parking lot with mud splashes on the windshield.

Your car is also the only one in the company parking lot that has an inch of dust inside and when you open the door, a swarm of flies emerge.

No one wants to ride in your car because they'll get sweet feed and hay in their socks and purses. That's ok because then you'd have to rearrange all the tack to make room for them, anyway!

You keep a spare curb chain in your purse for emergencies.

You have a small knife on your key chain.

You dress like a lawyer on weekdays and someone who needs a lawyer on your days off.

## The Aids

You're trying to get by a co-worker in a restricted space and instead of saying "excuse me" to him/her, you cluck at them instead.

When your horses, dogs, kids and husband all come to the same whistle!

You say "whoa" to the dog.

You say "whoa" to your kids.

You say "whoa" to your truck.

You yell at the kids, and the horse's name pops out.

You poke your honey in the ribs, saying, "over", in the kitchen.

You cluck to your car to get it to accelerate.

The bus driver misses your stop and you cry out WHOA.

You click your tongue and shout "come on" when passing a car.

You go around a turn a tad too fast and you say "eeeeeeeeezzzzz girl."

You half-halt your dog while out walking.

You change lanes while driving and your inside leg moves to apply pressure.

Your car skids on the ice. You try to leg yield it away from the ditch and back onto the road. And it works.

You practice transitions in the car during your commute, complete with seat aids and the occasional cluck to the car.

You take a corner just a tad too fast in your little sports car and you concentrate on not collapsing the inside hip.

You know you ride sidesaddle when: it's easier to drive stick, because you get to use your LEFT leg, too. And your right hand moves the "cane" (gear shift). it's easier to sit on the sofa's arm than the cushions. you walk into an antique store, see a fake hair bun, and think how useful that would be if you ever got your hair cut.

## Family

Your laundry consists of horse blankets, saddle pads, bandages, breeches, and lots and lots of dirty socks and everyone else in the house votes to give you your own laundry day after which you're required to clean out the machines because no one else can stand horse hair all over their clothes.

You have to eat a cold supper because the kettle is cooking a bran mash and the pan on the other burner is full of linseed.

You teach your sisters how to post on the arm of the couch before their first riding lesson.

You teach your little brother to skip by getting him to canter, then switch leads until he's doing one-tempi flying changes.

Your daughter is a horse person when she asks if she can wash her saddle pad with her clothes, because she doesn't have a full load and doesn't want her brother's clothes contaminating hers.

Your mother, who has no grandchildren, gets cards addressed to Grandma, signed by the horses and the dog.

Your horse eats before your husband!

Supper time is generally at 8:00 PM, and everyone has been home since before 5:00.

The horses get fed first. Actually, the horses are the only ones that you feed. Husband and kids fend for themselves.

Your husband brings the new saddle to bed so he can work on it while watching TV.

Your husband has absorbed so much horse terminology he refers to one of his basketball team's players as coming up lame.

You tell your husband he's going shopping because he needs to get shod.

After hugging your husband he says "is that a carrot in your pocket or are you happy to see me!"

The highlight of your day is working with your horses and your S/O. works by your side because it's the highlight of his day too.

You have the worming, lesson, and farrier schedules in your head, but frequently miss the kids' piano lessons, girl scouts, or changing the oil in the car.

You talk to the horses like they were kids.

You'd rather stay up with a friend's sick horse than babysit her kids.

Your 4-yr old son "honks" the horn on the western saddle and you spend five minutes trying to explain the purpose of the horn.

## Finance

You get your income tax refund and the first thing you do is head for the tack shop.

You spend more on that 6 year old jumper than you've EVER spent on a car!

You pay the farrier before the phone bill.

You pay the board bill before your mortgage.

You don't even want to think about how your car would be paid for, your mortgage would be much smaller, and you might have some savings if you didn't have horses.

You get to the checkout at the grocery and the only things you're buying are 5 gallons of corn oil and 10 pounds of carrots. Oh and maybe a frozen burrito if you have enough money left.

You spend $515 on plane fare, $314 on car rental, and stay at your former S/O's in order to ride your horse for a week.

You spend a lot of money on a trip to Europe and end up spending most of your time watching horses.

You buy lime and grass seed instead of the clothes you need for work.

You live hand to mouth and somehow come up with the $800 for emergency vet bills.

You buy watermelon when you don't even like watermelon so that you can give it to your horses.

For once you have extra money to buy yourself something, you get to the checkout counter, and decide that you don't really need that shirt anyway. The $25 could be an entry fee!

Your horse costs more than your truck or–if you're really committed–your house.

You realize that finding a horseshoe truly is lucky because you've saved ten bucks.

You can pinpoint anything you might need in 2 seconds in your tack trunk but seem to have misplaced this month's electric bill.

All your stock has 4 legs.

## Repairs

You buy duct tape by the case, and carry rolls in your pocketbook, briefcase, and the console of your car.

You patch your mud boots with duct tape and slog through knee-deep mud to get hay to your horse, who has commandeered the ONLY dry spot for miles.

Someone says, "Does anyone have a screwdriver?" and you hand them a hoof pick.

You start using baling twine to repair non-horse-related things.

You are one of the few people around that can fix "things" being used to repairing fences, etc that you horses have taken down.

## Grooming

You clean your tack after every ride but never ever wash the car.

Your horse gets more compliments for grooming than you do.

You keep a horse Grooma by the front door to get the horsehair off of your Levis after riding bareback.

You are totally grossed out by human hair in the sink or tub, but don't mind horse hair in your washer, on your clothes, or in your food.

You open the door to the closet where you keep your boots and the aroma of manure wafts out.

You horse has more kinds of shampoo and conditioner than you have.

You wonder if Hoofmaker doubles as a moisturizer.

Your horse gets new shoes more often than you.

You groom your horse daily and you haven't been to a beautician in months.

Your horse has its mane pulled more often than you get a haircut.

You often sneak furtively into Laundromats and pretend that you really didn't just put that stinky, filthy horse blanket into the comforter-sized machine.

You're buying clothes, and you choose them on the basis of whether you can wash horse slobber/manure out of them.

## Health and Medical Care

The doctor says the bump on your finger is an inflamed tendon sheath, and you tell him, "Oh, you mean a wind puff."

Your husband goes to the doctor with an attack of bursitis and you find yourself telling your friends: "The vet says he'll be on stall rest for a few days."

You tell your small animal vet that your cat's flea bite dermatitis looks like rainrot.

You're at work and you say the doctor hasn't called you back yet. Your co-worker says, "You or the horse?"

You explain to your child's pediatrician that you knew the child was sick because he was off his feed.

You not only have a writer's callus, but thumb and finger calluses from pulling your horse's mane. Not to mention calluses on your palms where the reins rest.

You are down and depressed and you go talk to your horse.

You call cramps a little colic.

You are eating lunch out, can continue to eat, not missing a mouthful, and discuss the surgery on a horse's leg and all the awful details.

You know you're a horse person when you talk about having a baby and people give you a really strange look and say, I didn't know you were pregnant. Oops! it's the four legged kind.

You see the vet more than you see your child's pediatrician.

Your horse gets vitamins and supplements every day. And you can't remember to take vitamins yourself.

You run your tongue over your back molars and idly wonder if they need to be floated.

## Horsey Gifts

You get all starry eyed over the new Millers catalogue instead of Victoria's Secret.

You don't have to be asked by your non-horsey family what you want for Christmas anymore. They now get their own State Line Tack catalogs.

Your S/O gives you a new pitch fork and a shovel for Christmas. You're thrilled. All your friends think you're wacky.

You are unreasonably pleased to get a horse item, ANY horse item, as a gift. "They really cared!"

You actually like all horse items, any horse items, regardless of execution.

You find it much easier to buy presents for you horsey friends than your non-horsey ones.

Every item on your own list to Santa can be picked up at the tack shop or the feed store.

You are browsing in a book store. You see a book call *Quantum Leap*. It takes a second for you to realize it's probably not about Grand Prix jumping especially given that you are looking in the Sci-Fi/Fantasy section.

## The Equine Lifestyle

One of your favorite smells in the world is horse sweat on leather

You know you're a horse person when your sole purpose in buying a five pound coffee can is to use as a grain can.

You save every horse magazine you have ever bought.

You wear NASCAR baseball caps to horse shows so people won't ask you questions that you can't answer.

You stay up until two in the morning walking a colicky horse whose name you don't know and whose owner you've never met.

You can't remember the word "heel" but instead refer to it as your "hock" (this is also done with other "parts" of the body, etc)

You tell a friend that you have to get home to feed your horse, which you do. This is done while your own stomach growls, because you haven't eaten all day. You than decide it won't take that much longer to clean a few stalls.

The only thing your friends, colleagues, and passing acquaintances can think of when they see you is "How are the horses?" or "How many horses do you have now?" or "Are you still riding?"

You leave work feeling stiff, tense, with indigestion or a headache, and all those feelings disappear the minute you go through the first gate to the ranch.

You feel tired all day at work and then go to the barn and ride 3 horses.

You arrive at the barn mad at the world, have an excellent ride on your horse, then go home feeling the world really is a pretty great place.

Every time you go to the stable, it takes 3 hours and you can't imagine where the time went.

You get a little whiff of manure smell and breathe deeper to get the full impact. That goes double for the smell of leather.

You pass up attractive social invitations because they conflict with your lesson schedule.

You've forgotten what a vacation is, because you spend all your paid time off (re)building fence, vet appointments, going to shows, etc.

You have a perpetually skinned place on your knuckles or the heel of your hand, from when the hoof rasp/pick slips.

Your friends and relatives stop asking when you're going to get married, and ask how the horse is instead.

Your boyfriend complains that you love your horse more then you love him and you answer: "And your point is?"

You tell a person "The mud was so deep it sucked the Tingleys right off!" and wonder why they give you a strange look.

You stop channel surfing at Budweiser Clydesdale commercials.

The sound of a hoof step or a whinny on the TV brings you dashing into the room. There you must stay until they show that horse again, and when they do you quickly analyze its breed, conformation, eye appeal, gender, attitude, level of training, and then decide if you would own it or not.

You pass a Marlboro billboard and immediately notice the horse's color, conformation, possible breed, gait, tack, bit, expression, and whether or not his mouth is being yanked on; but all you notice about the cowboy was that it was some guy in a rain slicker.

Books and movies are ruined for you if horsemanship references are incorrect.

Your horse thinks she's a dog, your dog thinks she's a cat, your cats think they are people, and you KNOW you were a horse in a former life.

You cannot imagine why anyone would think it kinky to own whips.

You are waiting in a parking lot and see a vacant Food Lion grocery store. By the time your husband has gotten back to the car, you've figured a way to make an awesome indoor arena out of it.

You answer and don't think twice about it when someone calls you your horse's name.

You are shopping and place the big package between your knees to hold it so you can read the magazine with both hands. And you know no one will think this is odd because you're in a tack store.

Your ideal birthday weekend extravaganza consists of going to two days worth of horse shows.

The most sincere hugs you give are to your horse.

You find dressage more interesting than show jumping.

All of your favorite stories involve your falls off horses, and other near death experiences and you actually LAUGH about the time you got dragged around the field by a spooked horse!

Someone sends you 400lbs of feed to sample.

Most of your social life is with other horse folk.

You get to a point where flies don't bother you so much.

## Living arrangements

You use the house-hunting trip your new employer provides to figure out where you will board your horse.

The real estate agent asks what kind of house you are looking for, and you say, "More than six acres."

You buy land and decide to build the barn before the house so your horses have a place to stay. Then you move into the barn yourself and forget about the house.

You build a garage that you're going to live in while you build the house, build a barn instead, and still live in a 1 room house after 11 years of marriage and (somewhat) gainful employment.

You live with electric fencing tape around the lawn, so the horses can mow it for you.

You buy about 15 lbs. of carrots a week, but wouldn't eat a carrot if somebody paid you.

Your house is "decorated" with bits, saddles, bridles, halters, blanket racks, trunks, trophies, and ribbons.

You've considered moving into the barn, since it is cleaner than the house.

The floor plan of the house you're building accommodates an equine lifestyle. Which means there is a cement-floored mud room with a drain in the center.

Repairing the loft door is a higher priority than replacing the front porch!

There are bits soaking in your bathroom sink.

There is at least one saddle in your living room.

There are neatsfoot oil stains on the carpet in front of the television.

## Maternity

You plan your pregnancy around the show season so you can send your horse to your dressage instructor for training during the eighth and ninth months.

You do stalls the morning before your labor is to be induced.

The doctor tells you that they have to do a C-section. Your first question (much to your spouse's horror) is "how long will it be until I can ride?" And you are devastated when she tells you 6 weeks.

Your daughter's birth announcement reads: "it's a filly!"

Your baby shower gifts include a fleece seat saver.

## Non-Horse People

A non-horsey co-worker asks how your horse is and you think: "she's not doing very well since you just changed to a milder bit but you want to give her a chance to get used to it.", and you say "Fine." Because you know if you say what you are REALLY thinking, by the time you're done, your co-worker will be sitting there with a blank look on her face.

After you just got stepped on, and a non-horse person asks you if you are alright, you say "what?" Not realizing what they are talking about.

Your non-horsey friend gives you a funny look after glancing into the back seat of your car, and you realize he's noticed your whips and spurs.

Your friends no longer ask to get together with you on a weekend afternoon because they know you'll say "I can't, I have to ride."

## Nutrition

You know more about equine nutrition than human nutrition and it shows.

You coax your horse into the trailer with a carrot, give him a bite, and walk out finishing it yourself. (family germ theory apparently extends to horses).

You go on a diet for your horse's sake, but not your S/O's.

You go on a diet, not to be more attractive, but to be a better rider.

Your horse gets vitamins and supplements everyday and you can't remember to take vitamins yourself.

## Photographs

You always have new foal pictures in your wallet.

The photo Christmas cards feature the horses.

You hate posing for pictures unless you're on your horse.

The only pictures in your office are of your horses.

The X-rated photo on your office wall is that of a gelding with his male member partly extended.

The family photos are in the bedroom; the horse photos in the den.

Folks ask incredulously how many horses you have, because your bulletin board at work is covered with 10 pictures of each horse and only a couple of your spouse or your kids (human, canine, or feline).

The only picture of you that your wife (husband, S/O, whatever) has of you shows you on your horse.

## Transportation

When the steering on your car starts to go out and all you can think about is how "stiff" the car is on one side.

You pull a $17,000 horse trailer with a $1,700 pickup truck.

You seriously consider trading your 2003 Buick for a 1992 diesel crew cab dually pickup truck, even swap.

You spend more time in your truck going to horse events than you spend at home.

You think they should outlaw air brakes on trucks.

You trade your yuppie mobile for a truck, so you can better accommodate your horses.

You try to book a seat at the Spanish Riding School BEFORE you buy your airline tickets because you'd rather change all your other plans than miss that show.

As you drive your car through the country, you evaluate fences and other obstacles for their jump-ability. How's the footing on the approach and landing? What line would I take? How difficult does it look?

The back of your station wagon is an auxiliary tack box.

You also know you're a h/j/ct person if you count strides to the beat of the music in your car and pretend that the telephone poles are the jumps.

You buy a pickup truck because you like it, and she puts a trailer hitch on it.

You count strides to the crack in the sidewalk, and then step over it.

You drive by any field anywhere and look very hard for horses. This includes trips to foreign countries.

You drive over potholes and practice sitting the trot while your car shakes over the road.

You hate shopping, but will drive 60 miles to check out a new tack shop.

You post over speed bumps.

You put a gun rack in your pickup truck to carry dressage whips and riding crops.

While jogging, your "inside" leg extends farther to help you balance.

Your car boot (trunk) and seats are permanently covered in hay and feed.

Your friends have to move your saddle or horse blanket out of the seat every time they get in your car.

Your truck looks like a bomb exploded in a tack shop.

You go to the gas station and ask the attendant to check the air in the "off hind." And you know you're in horse country when the young man immediately walks to the right rear tire!

## Weather

Your truck dies in the coldest part of the winter and you pick up hay in your Hyundai: six bales inside; four on the roof!

You'll drive an hour in a snowstorm to ride your horse, but God forbid you have to drive 1/2 hour to a friend's house for dinner.

After it snows, the pathway to the manure pile is the first thing that gets cleared, then the front porch and sidewalk.

You aren't interested in watching the news, but have to, in order to catch the weather, so you know if the barn needs to be left open for the horses.

You can't make it to work because of bad weather, but somehow still make it to the barn.

You don't think that weather is just casual conversation. It is very important so that you can figure out your horse's wardrobe for the day/night.

You drive 14 miles out and back in the rain in the morning to blanket your horse and then forget to take an umbrella to work.

You get out of your warm bed at 3:00 AM, and go outside to let the horses in because it's snowing (that wet, heavy stuff). If that's not enough, you scrape off the snow, and even dry them off a little, before going back to bed. Only to leave for work at 6, and see them back outside, with 2 inches of snow piled on their backs.

You'll drive an hour in a snowstorm to ride your horse, but God forbid you have to drive 1/2 hour to a friend's house for dinner.

You don't think that weather is just casual conversation. It is very important so that you can figure out your horse's wardrobe for the day/night.

On rainy days, you organize the tack room, not the house.

# You Know You are an Equestrian College Student When

---

You wonder why people complain about having to get up so early for a 9am class. You feel like saying, "Try getting up at 4am on weekends for horse shows!"

Your papers for your writing classes contain stories of horses.

When people complain about an instructor being cruel and too hard, you think of the riding instructors you've had: The ones who made you run the barrels on foot, jump bareback, or ride backwards to improve your balance.

If you have a MySpace account, it includes more photos of horses than of you.

You accept MySpace friends instantly if they have a picture of a horse in their profile.

You wonder why people buy energy drinks to get through their classes, when you spend early-mornings loading up horse trailers afternoons grooming horses, and, pulling all-nighters watching colicky horses. All on an empty stomach.

Your idea of a perfect boyfriend/girlfriend , besides being sweet, smart, and caring, and all that, is one who can muck stalls, stack hay, and enjoys riding on the beach.

You haven't been on a date in a long time and you think you'll probably end up marrying a farrier or a vet since they are the people you see most often.

In a human genetics class, you often ask things like, "Does it work like that in horses too?"

In biology class your instructor looks at you any time horses are mentioned.

Your instructor doesn't remember your name but calls you "the horse person."

In American History class, you often ask, "What was the name of his horse?"

When you write papers for history classes, you always mention the horses and their contributions to society.

You get excited in an English Literature class when you come across material about horses.

You've asked engineering students to calculate the wingspan of a hypothetically functional Pegasus.

You'd totally take the art class if, instead of sculpting a nude model, you practiced creating horses.

You write a movie review for literature class on Henry V and conclude it by analyzing the horsemanship in the film.

You see a cute guy and think, "I wonder what he'd look like in Wranglers?"

You ask your history teacher what the most important animal in history is and then argue with him that it was the horse.

You don't have a boyfriend/girlfriend because you spend all your spare time with your horses.

You can spend an hour discussing horses with an instructor or classmates, but not politics or sociology.

Your idea of a controversial issue is NAIS (National Animal Identification System), unwanted horses, or mustang management.

You don't understand mini-skirts or high-heeled shoes.

Someone complains of having to make a three hour drive, you smile and think of the time you drove nine hours to a clinic, or two days to make it to a horse show.

You have horse doodles in your notebooks.

You think the cafeteria food isn't THAT bad; You've had much worse at horse shows.

You see a girl wearing a pair of high-heeled, pointy-toed fashionable boots and when she tells you how much they cost you say, "Wow, you could have bought a nice pair of REAL boots for that!"

You end up driving your friends everywhere because your crew-cab dually can fit them all.

You've had to explain to said friends what some of the objects in your truck are; "That's a hoof pick..." "Umm, those leather strips are reins..."

You invite all your friends to come riding with you. This is all assuming you HAVE any friends because your horse takes up so much time.

You've answered your cell phone while riding and had to tell someone, "Hold on a second, my horse is being a brat."

The vet's number is programmed into your cell phone.

So is the farrier's.

You can't understand how people sleep till noon on the weekends; what a waste of productive early-morning time!

You can't understand why people can talk about cars for hours, but someone asks about your horse and you can't shut up.

You've spent more than an hour talking to someone at school about horses.

You've spent more than an hour talking to an instructor about horses.

You've walked up to strangers and joined in conversations because you heard them mention horses.

You tell your friends you can't make it because the farrier is coming and for a second don't realize why they look at you.

You frequently have to explain things to your non-horsey friends;"No, a pony is NOT a baby horse, A farrier has nothing to do with fairies. When I said I was training a stud, I meant a horse, stupid!"

You are one of the few people who can talk about whips, spurs, and leather and not think anything kinky.

Your arms and face are tanned, but your legs aren't.

You love the smell of horses, leather, and hay, but you've learned not to say that because people look at you weird.

You've called your horse your boyfriend/girlfriend or vice versa.

Your friends are going to a party over the weekend, but you can't make it because you have to muck the barn, stack hay, and move the sawdust pile.

You've spent calculus class explaining the barrel pattern to a friend and making them draw it.

You've asked instructors to write a letter of recommendation for you because you're applying for a horse scholarship.

You've asked an instructor if you could bring a horse to class for your presentation (in my case... they said yes!).

You've skipped class for a horse event.

Your research papers are about horses.

*Annamaria Tadlock, www.ultimatehorsesite.com*

# Ecstasy

You move your horse to a beautiful new stable on a bright, clear October afternoon and when you turn him out in that big, grassy field, he takes a look around him and takes off runnin' and a-buckin' and a-fartin' like he had never been out of a stall before. He's jest a big ol' bay horse until he gets that TB blood fired up and then he looks like the cover of King of the Wind (the book you checked out so much in elementary school the librarian cut you off). Nostrils flared, coat gleaming in the crisp air, and he's the most beautiful thing you've ever seen. When he's happy, he runs with his tail straight up in the air like an Arabian and your chest aches with happiness: this is the way it should be. He finds another TB and it's a match race!!!! I can get to the end of the field first!!! When you get home, your S/O asks you how the moving went. "Fine," you say, trying to think of the word that describes such a perfect moment. You give up. That word doesn't exist in any language.

# When I am old

I will wear soft gray sweatshirts

And a bandana over my silver hair

And I will spend my social security checks on wine and my horses.

I will sit on my porch in my well-worn chair

And watch my horses grazing.

I will sneak out in the middle of a warm summer night

And go for a horseback ride, if my old bones will allow.

When people come to call, I will smile and nod

As I show them my horses

And talk of them and about them

The ones so beloved of the past.

And the ones so beloved of today

I will work hard cleaning their stalls

Feeding them and whispering their names

In a soft, loving way.

I will wear the gleaming sweat on my brow

Like a jewel, and I will be an embarrassment to all.

Especially my family

Who have not yet found the peace in being free

To have your horses as your best friends.

These friends who always wait, at any hour, for your call

And eagerly run to the fence when they hear you

To greet you with nickers and neighs

With warm eyes full of adoring love and hope

That you will always stay.

I'll hug their big strong necks

I'll kiss their dear sweet muzzles

And they will love me in their special way.


I look in the mirror and see I am getting old

This is the kind of person I am

And have always been.

Loving horses is easy; they are a part of me

Please accept me for who I am, a horsewoman.

My horses appreciate my presence in their lives

When I am old this will be important to me

You will understand when you are old

If you have horses to love, too.

*Author Unknown*

# Finally . . .

---

How do you make a small fortune with horses? Start with a big one.

4940186R0

Made in the USA
Charleston, SC
08 April 2010